'If you wander off the road to the right or to the left you will hear His voice behind you saying, *THIS IS THE WAY, WALK IN IT.*'

Isaiah 30:21

A symposium to encourage those who are seeking to know God's will for their lives.

REAL GUIDANCE

REAL EXAMPLES OF GUIDANCE
TO HELP YOU LIVE YOUR LIFE

EDITED BY STEWART DINNEN

CHRISTIAN FOCUS/
WEC

ISBN 1-85792-668-4

© Copyright Stewart Dinnen 2003

Published in 2003
by
Christian Focus Publications,
Geanies House, Fearn, Tain,
Ross-shire, IV20 1TW, Scotland

www.christianfocus.com

and

WEC, Bulstrode, Gerrards Cross,
Bucks. SL9 8SZ, England.

Cover Design by Alister MacInnes

Printed and bound by
Cox and Wyman, Reading, Berkshire

Contents

* names have been changed to ensure confidentiality

Preface

There are two reasons for the publication of this book.

The first is that many young people have difficulties in discerning God's will and understanding the principles of guidance. I remember in the days of my own perplexity being greatly helped by a small IVF booklet entitled *Vocation* which was comprised of testimonies similar to these. A more recent book with very sound teaching called *Where do I go from here Lord?* (by Zac Poonen) has also helped meet the need for clear teaching on this subject.

But the second reason for its publication is to counter the effects of *Decision Making and the Will of God* by Garry Friesen. The writer tends to denigrate specific personal guidance and seeks to find scriptural substantiation for making decisions only on the broad general moral principles of the Word of God.

Knowing a great many missions and missionaries whose experiences completely demolish this denial of personal guidance, I felt that today's young people should have a sampling of such real-life proofs.

May these frank, fundamental testimonies be an encouragement to all readers to seek and find God's specific will for their lives.

Stewart Dinnen, Tasmania 2002

Introduction

The badge on his lapel had 'BAIK' so someone asked him what it stood for. He replied, 'It means, "Boy, am I Konfused."' 'But you don't spell "confused" with a K!' 'Oh, oh,' he replied, taken aback, 'Well, that only shows how confused I really am'.

Are you confused about God's call? I confess that I was for a long time. Some said, 'The NEED is the call'. Others said, 'Matthew 28:19 is the call'. Still another said, 'Every Christian is called to serve the Lord'.

Still not satisfied I began a careful study of Paul's call; here is what I saw:

1. He was clearly told that he would serve the Lord in specific kinds of Christian service. Acts 26:18 contains a number of activities.

* 'Open people's eyes, and turn them from darkness to light.' In other words he was to evangelize by proclaiming the gospel.

* He was to 'turn the people from the power of Satan to God'. That means he was to engage in a ministry of delivering people from any kind of bondage to which Satan had subjected them.

* Such people would 'receive forgiveness' and have a place 'among the sanctified'. This means that he was to be responsible for their spiritual growth to maturity.

Who can read Paul's letters and not agree that these three tasks were exactly what he did?

2. God gave him a sense of direction for such a ministry – it was to be to the Gentiles. This is clearly stated in 1 Timothy 2:7 and 2 Timothy 1:11. Even though he was a Jew he was specifically called to Gentiles.

3. The two Timothy references above also reveal his spiritual gifting. In both verses he states that these were preaching (or heralding), teaching, and apostleship (a mobile ministry of wisdom and counsel to churches and individuals).

Summarizing, Paul had:
* a commission to certain ministries,
* a sense of direction,
* a sense of gifting for the tasks given to him.

What are some of the tasks to be done in modern church life? These will include:

Evangelizing	Teaching
Pastoring	Leading small groups
Counselling	Administration
Visiting	Radio script writing
Practical service	Social service
Youth & children	Preparing videos, etc.

And when we think of cross-cultural service, all of these, plus:

Building	Medical work
Literature	Rural development
Leadership training	Agriculture
Motor engineering	Communications
Education, etc.	

Examining Paul's experience of guidance more closely still, we can see from Acts 13 that the Holy Spirit has impressed him directly with a sense of call ('...for the work to which I have called them' verse 2). But the Holy Spirit also dealt with the leaders of the Antioch church ('...set apart for me Barnabas and Saul'). Also note that they were not sent out by the leaders – they were sent by the Holy Spirit. The word used for the function of the leaders was not to 'send', as in most versions, but to RELEASE.

The leaders' laying on of hands was a symbol of identification with the missionaries – a point which should not be lost in today's churches when workers are sent out. If you are a member of an evangelical church it seems biblical to seek the leaders' commendation and counsel before moving out.

How are we to distinguish between the leading of the Spirit and our own feelings or desires? Generally the pressure from the Holy Spirit is steady, not varying in intensity. Human feelings can be very variable and subject to changes in moods and circumstances. The key to being able to distinguish between the two is the quality of our daily walk with the Lord, as prescribed by Jesus in John 15.

Circumstances on their own do not constitute guidance; it is how we interpret them that is important, and this, again, goes back to the state of our personal relationship with the Lord and the degree of sensitivity we have to Him. If God wants you in Christian service you can be sure Satan doesn't, and he will do all he can to hinder and discourage you.

1

The Specific Word of the Lord

Out of the drug culture
Elliot Tepper/Spain

It is difficult for me to separate the call of God from the call to missions. Moments before I surrendered my life to Christ in the emergency room of a Boston hospital the Lord said two things to me. First He asked me, 'Why are you dying?' and then He said, 'I want you to live and have many children'. Without answering His question or understanding the declaration that followed, I repented and opened my heart to the love of God. After that encounter with Christ my life changed radically. The Lord plucked me up out of the drug culture and set me down among godly Christians in North Carolina.

During the first year of my Christian life I was quite content to be saved, and entertained no thought of service to God other than perhaps a vague idea that one day I might become a Christian writer. I began to attend a small church called the Seagate Community Chapel in Wilmington. One evening an old missionary named A.S. Worley came to speak. I can remember him talking about his ministry among the tribes of New Guinea and our responsibility to take the Gospel to the uttermost parts of the earth. He told about the time he had preached for four hours to a group of stone age tribesmen, and when he had finished preaching another tribe came walking up to the church. He was told that they had walked three days to hear the Gospel and was asked if he would please preach again. He could not say 'no' and preached another four hours. After hearing that message I have never been the same. I believe it was at this time that God put the general call to be a missionary in my heart and, with it, the desire to make known the Gospel where it has never been preached before.

Shortly after this, persuaded that the Lord wanted me to be a missionary, I enrolled in the Faith Training Centre Missionary Institute in South Carolina where A.S. Worley was the president. My life was greatly enriched and my concern for missions deepened. However, my burden was not for any particular country, but for the whole unevangelized world.

After one semester I married and left the Institute. My wife, Mary, and I naïvely felt that at any moment we would hear God's specific call and then He would launch us out into world missions. After a year of working, waiting and being faithful in a local church I was frustrated, so I decided to fast and seek the Lord's direction.

A word from the Lord

One day while I was fasting someone called us on the telephone and said, 'There is a minister speaking at a nearby church; I think you ought to hear him. The gifts of the Spirit are operating in his life.' The Lord moved upon my heart to take her advice and visit a church where I had never been before and listen to a minister completely unknown to me. We arrived and entered the service. He and his family were singing. When they stopped he said to the congregation, 'Costa Rica, no... Costa Deir. Is there anyone here who knows Costa Deir?' I was the only soul who knew this man and raised my hand. Then the minister said, 'I don't know what this means, but I believe he has a word of guidance for you'. The heavens opened and the Holy Spirit fell upon me in power and with great peace. I knew God was saying something, but what exactly, I knew not.

We went home that night and I wrote a letter to Costa Deir who was the foreign missionary secretary for the Elim Fellowship in Lima, New York. I simply recounted what had happened. He sent me a very short letter which said, 'This is God. You come here.'

On the strength of the minister's 'word of knowledge' (see 1 Cor. 12:8), Brother Deir's confirmation, and the peace and conviction in our hearts, we closed our home in North Carolina and moved to Lima, New York, where we entered Elim Bible Institute. Elim is a great crossroads of faithful service and missionary activity. During our two-and-a-half years in the Elim family our vision of the purposes of God was enlarged and our calling to missions deepened. Up to this point we still had no specific focus. The specific call eluded us. We finished our course without receiving a clear word of guidance and then returned to North Carolina where I served for almost a year as an assistant pastor in our church. We were a bit perplexed and frustrated. I had heard God's general call to missions five years earlier and we had taken bold steps of faith to move towards the fulfilment of it, but still did not have His specific commission. Through hindsight I can understand why God held us back. It was not that He was delaying us, but rather renewing us, stabilizing us and preparing us for our life's calling.

A specific call

One day a missionary from Mexico came to speak. He and I had been class mates at Faith Training Centre. While I had left Faith Training Centre to marry, work, attend Elim Bible Institute, and enter the pastorate, he had taken his family directly to Mexico as independent faith missionaries. The Lord had mightily used him, first to help found a thriving church in Mexico City and then later to preach the Gospel in dozens of villages in the mountains of Southern Mexico. I can remember sitting in our kitchen, listening to him share about the hunger for God among the unreached Mexicans and their wholehearted response to the Gospel. My heart burned within me simply listening to his stories. One evening he turned to me and said, 'How old are you?' I replied, 'Thirty-one.' Then he said, 'If you don't go to the mission field this year, you'll never go'. I was smitten. I felt as if the Lord had sent a prophet into our midst. In that moment He sent the shaft of His arrow into my heart with a specific call to Mexico. My friend made it clear that we would be welcome to work with him there and that he would help us get established in the Mexican culture.

Finally, with a specific word from God to our spirits, we felt we could now move out in faith. But first we presented our plans to the senior pastor and the elders of the church, trusting that they would confirm our calling. The elders gave us their blessing, but to our chagrin the pastor did not. In fact, he was emphatic and made it very clear that our place was in North Carolina as his assistant in a growing church that needed our ministry. He told us in no uncertain terms that if we went to Mexico we would be out of the will of God. This development put us in a very difficult situation because by persuasion we were committed to the Biblical principles of collective counsel and submission to pastoral authority. We were not rebels at heart. During that difficult time our call was tested, but the Lord upheld us and assured us that 'we ought to obey God rather than men' (Acts 5:29). We quietly and humbly left the church and made plans to head for Mexico without any guaranteed support. The Lord miraculously supplied all our needs and graciously blessed our four years of ministry there. We never lacked any good thing.

In our last year I began to sense a longing in my spirit to move on. Our ministry was fruitful. We had already helped establish a new church in Cholula Puebla and were experiencing a small revival among the students at the University of the Americas. We had a group of about twenty converts meeting regularly in our home. The Lord had even used our lives to touch some of the faculty and administration with the Gospel. There was no human reason to move on, yet the Holy Spirit was tugging at our hearts.

Another word from God

One day while in Mexico City I was returning a film I had borrowed from Wayne Myers, a grand old missionary with nearly forty years of experience. As we chatted he mentioned that his son and daughter were preaching the Gospel in Spain. He began to talk about the great need of the Spanish people. There were over 38,000,000 Spaniards and only about 40,000 evangelicals, making Spain one of the least evangelized nations in the world. He said, 'Since Franco's death Spain is wide open to missionaries, but the people's hearts remain closed to the Gospel'. When I left his home that day, I left with a weighty burden on my heart that would not go away.

Shortly after that encounter the biography of C.T. Studd, by Norman Grubb, fell into my hands. My spirit leapt as I poured over the pages. Here was a man and a mission that daringly, through faith, chose to walk in the heights of discipleship. I sensed in C.T. Studd's life the same notes I had heard at Faith Training Centre and Elim: faith, holiness, sacrifice, and fellowship. Perhaps the quality of heroic sacrifice appealed to me most. In any case, I felt impressed to write WEC a letter asking for an application. They sent me a preliminary form and invited me for an interview at Fort Washington, Pennsylvania. That summer we made a trip to the States. On the way we stopped at Faith Training Centre and I asked for Brother Worley's counsel concerning our decision to apply to WEC. I waited for his response as he sat slowly rocking in his chair on the porch overlooking the school grounds. He said nothing for a few moments, then he carefully said, 'I've known many WEC missionaries. It is the best mission in America.' Then he paused and thought a little longer and said with conviction, 'No! They are the best missionaries in the world!' I had always valued Brother Worley's counsel and rejoiced to know that he felt we were on the right track.

The word confirmed

Shortly afterwards, I had my interview with Duane Olson, the candidate secretary in Ft Washington. As we talked I can remember him saying, 'We have examined your papers and think that tentatively Spain might be the best field for you'. After my interview I headed for Pittsburgh where I was to spend a few days ministering at the Church of the Risen Saviour. I had decided to make a quick side trip to New Castle to visit Mrs Claudia Miller, a dear old saint, who in her 90s still interceded daily for missionaries. She lived with her Bible open on her lap and prayed continually. I had said nothing to Mrs Miller about Spain or my intention to leave Mexico, or of my interview with WEC the day before. When she opened the door of her home we greeted one another. The first words to come out of her mouth were, 'Pray about going to Spain. I believe God wants you in Spain.' Then she handed me a picture of King Juan Carlos and invited me to lunch. If I had had any doubts before, they were gone. I knew I could say like Paul, 'But now having no more place in these parts... I take my journey into Spain' (Rom. 15:23, 24).

After twenty-five years as missionaries in Mexico and Spain we are more than ever certain that we have made the right decisions in obeying the inner voice of the Spirit. The Lord has honoured each step of faith we have taken, and blessed us not only with an ever-present sense of the divine vision, but with abundant visible fruit. Firstly, out of our little group in Cholula, Mexico, at the University of the Americas, has come the 4,500 member Amistad de Puebla congregation. Secondly, out of the meetings in our home in Madrid has come the continually growing number of churches and rehabilitation communities of Betel that are flourishing in over fifty cities in ten countries of the world.

We are persuaded that the Lord delights to guide His people and that as we abide in union with Christ our ears shall hear a word saying, 'This is the way, walk ye in it' (Isaiah 30:21).

2

We're not after an easy life

P. M. JOHN, India/Ghana/Singapore

Dedicated at two

It is a marvel to me that God called me to the
mission field. I have always felt that I am
unworthy of such a great honour. I often like
to read Isaiah 41:14 with my name inserted
instead of Jacob. 'Do not be afraid O worm
John... for I myself will help you, declares the
Lord.'

I was born and bred in a village family in the
south of India. My parents were Christians and
belonged to the Syrian Christian community of
Kerala. When I was seven my father died and I
grew up with a tremendous inferiority complex.
My childhood was a time of many revival
meetings among the Marthoma Syrian
Christians where I was often taken by my
mother. I was also regular in Sunday School and
church services. During this time the Word of
God was sown deeply into my heart. This really
became the basis of God's call to me in later
years.

There was another thing that influenced me
very much. When I was two, a prominent
Marthoma priest held a series of meetings in the

village parish to which my father and mother regularly went. I was taken along too. In one of those meetings the priest asked for children to be dedicated to God's service. My father, prompted by the Holy Spirit, I believe, dedicated me to the Lord then. Even though my mother told me about this when I grew older she did not seem to have taken it to heart after father died. I did not think about it seriously either, even though at the back of my mind there was always a feeling that I was chosen to serve God.

I had my primary and secondary school education in the village. Those days were really quite humdrum, and I was an average student. Mother worked hard to bring us up well and since there were only three children in the family she was able to manage. We had enough food most of the time and new clothes at the beginning of the school year. Some years we even had new things at Christmas time as well. Outwardly everything seemed to be fine but though I was very religious, inwardly I was very insecure and unhappy.

Blessings in Allahabad
It was in this frame of mind that I went to university in a North Indian town called Allahabad. Here through divine providence, I came into contact with the EU (Evangelical Unions). I was greatly blessed in my spiritual life through my association with this group.

While in college I never really considered full-time work although it was always there somewhere at the back of my mind. However, I became more involved in the EU activities and held several offices in it including the presidency during my final year at college.

I did a degree in agriculture and when I left, my mother and older brother who had supported me wanted me to get a well-paid job and help them financially. I too had the same intention. But God's plans were different.

In the months just after I left college and while waiting for a job, the Lord turned my attention to the many young people in the village who did not know the Saviour. The Lord laid a tremendous burden on me for these people. They appeared to me as sheep without a shepherd. I was naturally shy and I still had quite a bit of my childhood inferiority complex. But this burden within me pushed me out to share the gospel with them. Many were saved both from nominal Christian and Hindu backgrounds. Eventually a group of Christian young people was formed for Bible study, prayer and witness. This group in the village went on for many years even after I left, and produced many fine Christians and spiritual leaders.

Vision expands

The formation of the group gave me tremendous joy and widened my vision. The Lord began to lay on me a burden for young people in other places too. At this time a door was opened for me to become a staff worker of the Union of Evangelical Students of India (UESI). My job was to work among the students in the state of Kerala. When I was faced with the decision to step out into full-time Christian work, I was afraid. Opposition began to rise up, too.

First of all I began to say, 'Lord I really have no special talents and when it comes to public speaking I just can't do it'. This was not a lame excuse, it was true. Even today this is how I feel. I sometimes feel a bit cross with the Lord for not giving me any special talents. But then of course, you know what the Lord always says when you say that, 'My grace is sufficient for you'. That is what the Lord said to me when I first considered full-time ministry. The passage the Lord used was from Jeremiah 1:4-10. The words, 'Before I formed you in the womb I knew you, and before you were born I consecrated you, I appointed you a prophet to the nations' came to me ever so strongly and confirmed the deep conviction that I was meant to be in full-time ministry. I'm sure this is connected with the action of my father who dedicated me to the service of God when I was only two years old.

My objections were like Jeremiah's, but the Lord said, 'Do not say "I am only a youth" for to all to whom I send you you shall go and whatever I command you you shall speak. Be not afraid of them for I am with you to deliver you.' These words have been a source of great strength to me ever since and the basis of all my future decisions.

So the first objection which was from within myself was resolved. But then there were others from outside. The greatest was from the family. My mother and brother were very much against my joining an organization that could not even pay me enough money to live on. They had financed my education; now it was my turn to earn money and support them. It was a hard choice for me; they did need my help but the call of God was so strong, nothing they said could now deter me from following Him.

Most of my friends did not understand me either. Some said I was crazy to forsake my good training to join a fanatic religious organization. Some even said I was mad. But now that I was sure that it was God who was calling me, I would only smile at all these reactions.

So, I joined the UESI in 1970. As far as my family was concerned, the Lord proved His goodness by blessing them in various ways even though I was not able to give them anything.

I worked with the UESI three years during which time I felt very much the need for greater knowledge of the Word of God. So in 1973 I went to the Discipleship Training Centre in Singapore for a two year Bible training course.

It was while I was there that I met Mr Leslie Brierley of WEC International and learned a bit about the great worldwide spiritual need. At that time the Lord began to plant in me seeds of interest in world missions. Of course, it was not a question of whether I wanted to be a missionary now. I was willing to go anywhere; it was only a question of knowing where He wanted me to be. At the end of my training in Singapore the Lord directed me back to India.

Africa in the picture

I started to develop an interest in Africa and I began to ponder the possibility of going there with a secular agency, and doing missionary work as well. As I had qualified as an agriculturist there was a possibility of going with the United Nations. The idea of going as a full-time missionary through a western mission society did not occur to me. I really did not think it was possible. And there were no Indian societies which sent missionaries to Africa. But when I saw an article in the *Look* missionary news digest (produced by WEC), asking for agriculturists to go to Africa as missionaries, I was prompted to write and offer myself. The reply was very encouraging but I was told that I was going to be a 'guinea pig' since I was the first Indian to apply to WEC for cross-cultural missionary work. Looking back now I think the experiment, as far as we were concerned, went well.

After contacting WEC in 1976 there was a long period before I finally arrived in Ghana. There was the long correspondence first. Then my marriage to Wabang in 1978. The subsequent arrival of our first son delayed our joining the mission quite a bit. There was also the question of which sending base we should join. There was no WEC headquarters in India and nowhere near for us to do our candidate course. Finally it was decided that we should attend the course in Britain and be sent out from there, so we joined the candidate course in February 1980.

At this time too there were many misunderstandings. Many friends said that I was an escapist trying to get away from the problems in India. Others said that we were opportunists trying greener pastures for making more money. This latter criticism had much weight since gospel work in many cases had become an 'industry'. Many people go to western countries, especially to America, in the name of gospel work and come back with fat bank balances, drive around in expensive cars and put up large buildings for their own use. This indeed is deplorable. Therefore, not many people understood us or identified with us.

Consciences clear

We faced this same criticism later on from western Christians too. A recent comment from a mission leader classified all Indians as not capable of living sacrificially. To him all Indians can be included in the saying, 'When an Indian nun takes the oath of poverty, she is in reality making sure of a square meal a day'. But our consciences were clear that we were neither after wealth nor an easy life. The Lord has helped us to live simply and we have tried not to be selfish with the things God has given to us.

There was also the practical problem of our financial support. It was impossible for us to take any money out of India because of governmental restrictions. But the Lord wonderfully raised a church in Britain which partially supported us. The members have been a tremendous spiritual encouragement to us ever since.

Once we reached Africa we had very few problems adjusting to the African culture. There are many similarities between the two. We probably had more difficulty adjusting to our missionary colleagues!

Five tribal churches raised
One question we were asked both before and after we joined WEC was, 'Why leave home and go elsewhere while there is a great need in India itself?' My primary answer to that is that the need does not constitute the call. God has a specific purpose for each of our lives and to find that out is more important than to be buried in something that we consider of greater importance. In my case it began with a gentle

impression in my mind that God wanted me to be a missionary in Africa. I was absolutely willing to obey God's will whatever it was. So I began pursuing this interest and God began to open doors. This was circumstantial evidence that I was in the right direction. Then the four years of uncertainty and delay did not dim the interest. By the way in which the Lord led us at each step we were absolutely convinced that this was God's will for us.

Secondly, I believe that the co-operation and fellowship of all believers all over the world, is necessary for the speediest evangelization of the world. Therefore I do not feel second rate being a missionary from a third world supported by a western church. I am happy to be in the centre of God's will!

As we evaluate our time in Ghana we believe God took us there. We have been instrumental along with national workers in the establishment and growth of five fellowships amongst a tribe that had been traditionally resistant to the Gospel.

[In 1989 the Johns were elected leaders of WEC's Ghana field. They have recently completed a five year stint as candidate directors at the Singapore base.]

3

It's a long way from Banga to Betel

Myk McKenzie, Spain/Italy

A canoe was better than a car

'But God, what will they think when I tell them
I'm going to a MISSIONARY training college?
You know that people have such weird ideas of
what a missionary is. They won't understand.
Besides, I love nursing. And how am I going to
live without a wage? I can't stand the idea of
having to depend on others financially. And
another thing, Lord, You know I want to marry.
If I become a missionary the chances of doing
so look very slim indeed. I'm scared.'

These questions and a score of others coursed
through my mind as I wandered home after
work. Only one month earlier the Lord had
dropped the long-awaited yet skilfully avoided
bombshell, 'Well, Myk, how long are you going
to remain here? How about Missionary Training
College now?'

Born in the British Solomon Islands, where
my parents worked with the New Zealand
Methodist Mission, I was more at home in a
canoe than a car. We children enjoyed a full and
fascinating childhood running about barefooted

on the tropical isle of Banga, where Dad was the school headmaster. A few tropical creatures and illnesses, sunburn and terrifying nightmares disturbed an otherwise idyllic situation for three inquisitive kids. I still vividly remember the snakes we deliberately kept in the rafters slithering after shrieking rats while I lay thankful for the mosquito net over my bed below.

But life abruptly changed course for me when, at the age of eight, my parents accepted my grandparents' invitation to care for me and to send me to school back in New Zealand. Besides, mum now had her hands full teaching us by correspondence and coping with new twin babies (after losing the last baby). I'll never forget the traumatic parting!

Mum, Dad, Bev, Russ and toddling Rod and Stu joined me ten months later. Leaving Hamilton, we went to live in Bombay, thirty miles south of Auckland. Dad plunged into Bible translation, preaching and fathering his family, baby Shirl having made her entrance. They had buried two newborns. But these were happy days, living as a close-knit family.

Brisbane and Billy Graham
Then Dad was offered a scholarship by the Queensland University to work on Aboriginal languages in Australia. So we packed up yet again and made our new home in St Lucia, Brisbane. The typically Queensland-style home on stilts,

with its tongue and groove woodwork and huge
verandah was purchased without our even seeing
it and to this day continues to stand as proof of
God's care.

I was fourteen, and city life combined with
the pressures of high school and adolescence
produced a rebellious teenager who made life
difficult for the family. Fortunately, at the age
of fifteen a frustrated Myk was cornered by God
at a city-wide Billy Graham Crusade. I
reluctantly admitted that I was not sure if I was
going to heaven. With my heart pounding I
made sure! I asked Jesus to save me and be my
Lord. The relief I experienced resulted in a new
boldness. Lyn Gallagher, on the staff at
Toowong High School, was instrumental in my
spiritual growth as I now threw myself into Inter
School Christian Fellowship and other activities
without fear of what my peer group would
think.

Nurse Rushton Hall was the call-name I
proudly bore when I began nursing at the
Princess Alexandra Hospital. (Mum and her six
'Rushton' sisters had been nurses.) With the first
pay I bought my first dress and gave the
remainder to a needy friend. In spare time I sang
in a Christian folk-rock group and helped with
Nurses Christian Fellowship activities. The Lord
Jesus, as my daily Companion, made the Bible a
practical guide as I worked on the hospital wards,

helping patients and staff to find spiritual as well as physical health. God and I grew closer.

My initial brush with WEC came when I began midwifery training at the Queen Victoria Maternity Hospital in Launceston, Tasmania. I probably went out to the college as much for the male company as for the spiritual home it was to become to me. A term caring for the children in the creche, after my course was over, put in me a desire to experience in a deeper way what I observed in those happy months – a caring family, a spiritual yet highly practical lifestyle, a 'high calling'. But I was not ready.

It was while living in a caravan with my sister Bev, anxiously awaiting work in Maryborough, Queensland, that God began to open my eyes to the faith-rest principle in daily life – another stepping stone in my growth to total dependence on Jesus.

Growth in the Outback

A third certificate, that of Maternal & Child Health, gave me the opportunity to live on the Health Department's service railcar, based in Hughenden, NW Queensland. Living on the railway and sharing my life with the isolated and scattered families along the track gave me almost a year to grow in God. Then it was home to Brisbane and operating theatre work at the nearby Wesley Hospital. Imagine my thrill on receiving a letter of thanks from Stepheny, the nurse who had succeeded me on the railcar. We had shared three weeks together and the day after I left, she cried out to the visiting pastor who 'happened' to call by, 'Nev, how can I know God?' She gave her life to Christ there and then. We still keep in touch.

Now the Lord faced me up with the decision to burn all my bridges behind me and to 'launch out into the deep'. To be honest, I went through a time of depression which even affected relationships with my family – later to be confessed and forgiven. The 'letting go' of the so-called security I enjoyed in my profession, family and friends was subtly and severely challenged by the enemy, the Devil. A timely caution from Evan Davies, Principal of WEC's Missionary Training College, helped: 'Don't be surprised if Satan counters your decision, Myk'.

I must admit that I felt weak in faith and like Gideon asked God to show me in some tangible way that it was HIM that I was hearing. I asked for three verses in three consecutive quiet times in the Bible passages I was currently studying, to rebuke the fears and doubts that faced me. He gave them to me. Specifically they allayed my fears of 'leaving all', of what people were saying, and of knowing God's timing. Here they are:

'Yes', Jesus replied, 'and everyone who has done as you have, leaving home, wife, brothers, parents or children for the sake of the Kingdom

37

of God, will be repaid many times over now, as well as receiving eternal life in the world to come.' Luke 18:29.

'So, my dear brothers, since future victory is sure, be strong and steady, always abounding in the Lord's work, for you know that nothing you do for the Lord is ever wasted as it would be if there were no resurrection.' 1 Cor. 15:58.

'This time I don't want to make just a passing visit and then go right on; I want to come and stay a while, if the Lord will let me.' 1 Cor. 16:7.

Spirited to Spain

And He DID let me! As a student at MTC in 1979 and 1980, I sampled real community life. Rubbing shoulders with so many characters and nationalities meant dealing with pride, jealousy, grudges, independence, selfishness and lack of transparency. Together we learnt not just ABOUT God and His Word, but to KNOW HIM, the Person, the God of all time and history. Our eyes were opened to new views and fresh forms of worship; the globe became a meaningful world of fascinating people, places and needs; prayer reached a level of KNOWING that the answer was already there; some of us were freed to demonstrate love and care in a new way; what I expected to be boring subjects instead whetted my appetite for learning; I even quietly fell in love, but the endless flow of visiting missionaries throwing out the challenge of the whitened harvest was the bait I needed.

Nevertheless, there loomed one big problem... 'WHERE, LORD? WHERE in this big, needy world do I fit?' Actually, I'd always inwardly expected to end up in deepest, darkest Africa... after all, my early childhood and nursing training obviously pointed to that! Eventually, in desperation, I sat down and scribbled my thoughts. I came to the surprising realization that, for the past sixteen years I'd actually been involved in URBAN activities within church, school, music, outreaches, NCF, etc. Gradually the mountain of possible 'spots' shrank as I constantly talked to God, shared my thoughts with older and wiser Christians and generally kept heading towards a cross-cultural ministry.

I've never been 'zapped' by an unmistakable 'heavy word' regarding Spain – the land from which I now pen these lines. Rather, it was more a case of little things, coupled with a quiet excitement (but not without apprehension!) assuring me that I was headed in the right direction. I shared every single thought with the Lord constantly.

I can never thank God sufficiently for having brought me here to Spain. My life is now SO much richer in God for having left what I had imagined to be the 'indispensable'. Mind you, it has not been easy. But starting afresh in a foreign country, culture and language was just what my independent self needed. I've known what it is to have little and also to have more than I've needed, but I've never felt abandoned by my Heavenly Father.

Singleness and satisfaction

How did I cope with singleness? Not too well at times. Like most girls I indulged in a regular weep, but the Lord always hugged me happy again; being busy and satisfied in work helped. Getting out of the flat, rather than moping at home, washing my hair or having a spring clean generally did the trick. And deep inside me lingered the hope that Lindsay McKenzie, whom I'd secretly fallen in love with at MTC, and whom God had brought to Spain a year after me, would be God's choice.

Seven years passed from our first meeting before he received a tap on the shoulder from the Lord confirming to him that he was to ask me to marry him. Of all places, Lindsay chose a busy supermarket during a rushed shopping trip. You could have knocked me over with a feather! Of course I said YES!

Many have quizzed the long wait. But God's timing is ALWAYS perfect. I know that I must never manipulate in any way. Lindsay knew that he had to find his total satisfaction in God first, and that included finding his niche in ministry. Looking back we thank the Lord for the fabulously full and infinitely invaluable years we enjoyed as 'singles'. We had now to learn to serve Him together as a couple – not as simple a process as we'd imagined!

Rescue shop

Raúl Casto and the six other heroin-addicts Lindsay had taken into his small highrise flat in San Blas, Madrid, moved out to a more roomy farmhouse and I moved in. Sharing the care of the church (begun in the home of our team leaders, Elliott and Mary Tepper) and Drug Rehabilitation/Discipleship Centre (begun in Lindsay's flat), plus prison visitation, kept us on the stretch. Elliott chose the name BETEL for this ministry. (You can read the exciting story of BETEL's birth and growth in *Rescue Shop* by Stewart and Marie Dinnen.)

On returning from our first furlough we found ourselves 'without a job', in the right sense. The men and women we had discipled were now discipling others and doing a better job than we had! We obviously had to move out and let them get on with the development of the mother work. With a team of four men we moved east to open up the Valencia province. BETEL Valencia now has a church functioning alongside the Rehabilitation Centre. This pattern of multiplication has been duplicated in scores of places both inside and outside of Spain over the last thirteen years.

We have just completed five years of service in Italy during which God has touched many lives and raised up four Betel centres in Naples, Bari, Genoa and Catania in Sicily.

4

An offering of gratitude

Sylvia Brynjolfson, Argentina/Equatorial Guinea/Canada

African adventure

As we approached the coast we could finally relax. The two hours in the narrow canoe were so stressful. I was constantly grabbing our two children (1 and 3 years old) who tottered about. On one side of the river was Gabon, and on the other Equatorial Guinea – the country in Central Africa where the Lord had given fruitful ministry.

Although we turned toward land, the dugout still had to take us through a labyrinth of narrow river channels like fingers of water stretching into the jungle. The kids were delighted with the crabs and walking fish running into their holes in the mud as we passed by. Eventually, the water became too shallow for the canoe. The remainder of the muddy channel was traversed on foot carrying the kids and luggage to dry ground.

This kind of 'adventure' was nothing new for my husband Rob. He frequently travelled in the interior of Equatorial Guinea doing evangelism. But I was delighted. This was the first long journey that we could take as a family now that the kids were at a more suitable age. I had been invited to speak at a ladies' convention of the WEC-related churches.

We still had a trek of several kilometres before we reached the village but the solid ground was appreciated. Our kids were easily distracted, stopping frequently to enjoy the different sights, sounds and fruit they had never seen in the city. The sound of the drums of the welcoming reception made us speed up. I was overwhelmed and humbled. During the convention the Lord manifested Himself in a supernatural way bringing reconciliation, healing, deliverance and repentance through the Word proclaimed.

I returned with unspeakable joy through the same jungle, mud and water. Since we still had a long drive I was able to review and evaluate the expectations I had brought to this conference. I asked myself, as I often did when the Lord manifested Himself in a powerful way, 'Who am I to have the privilege of serving the Lord in Africa?' As I looked back on my life I saw that it was like a big chess game in which the Lord moved people and changed circumstances with great precision.

Argentina
Missionaries...! I knew lots of them. They spoke in English to their kids. They preached with an

accent. They taught us to drink tea and they went to picnics dressed in a suit and tie. That was my earliest image of what a missionary was. My parents were committed Christians before I was born. I grew up in a Brethren congregation in Santa Fe, Argentina that was richly blessed by resident and visiting missionaries who shared their passion for the Word.

I came to know the Lord at the age of eight and it wasn't long before I was teaching children in different outreaches that our church had around the city. But it wasn't until I was eighteen that I was confronted with the reality of the power of the Gospel to change lives.

Uncertainty about my future and spiritual crisis dampened the excitement of finishing high school. Yet, the Lord intervened. I joined a musical group with 'Youth for Christ' and travelled around some countries in South America. In Lima after finishing the meetings in a church we went out with the young people. Some started to share their testimonies. Ex-drug addicts and guerillas were telling how Jesus had changed their lives. I had only heard about things like this happening. My whole life was shaken. The uncertainty about my future left as I dedicated my life to the Lord. I returned home determined to go to Bible School.

The next four years at the Instituto Biblico in Buenos Aires opened my eyes to see the riches of Biblical truth and gave me a hunger to continue in this area. Uncertainty about my future followed graduation. I had only one thing in mind – to continue biblical studies. There were no higher level studies available in Argentina at this time, but the Lord intervened unexpectedly. My father decided to apply for a Canadian Landed Immigrant visa on behalf of the whole family. When he was accepted we were all shocked. In a few months we had to sell our family business and possessions.

Once in Vancouver, in the midst of my struggles with a different language and culture, I started to study at Regent College. The three year course produced an effect similar to the previous biblical studies in Argentina: a deepening of the knowledge of the Lord enriched and expanded my love for Him and stimulated my desire to serve Him.

Things start to come together
During those years my family and two Canadian missionary couples participated in the formation of a Spanish-speaking church. I was very challenged by their passion for the Lord and for other people. My only desire was to be like them one day.

On a cold and snowy December evening I approached one of these couples – Wilfred and Elizabeth Watson, former workers in Venezuela – in a coffee house in downtown Vancouver. (Once a week we presented a programme trying to reach the newly arrived political refugees from Central America.) I shared with them my desire to become a missionary and they told me about their mission – WEC. Right away I had the feeling that I was going in the right direction.

In that same coffee house I met Rob, who had just come back from serving the Lord in Bolivia and was interested in practising his Spanish. I enjoyed chatting in Spanish with this handsome, mission-minded guy, asking myself who would be the lucky girl that would marry him. Certainly not I, it would seem – our lives were going in different directions. Rob was determined to go back to Bolivia and I was heading for Spain, convinced of the gigantic need of that country.

Anyway, I applied to WEC, completed the candidate course in Hamilton, Ontario, and was accepted for Spain.

Just before my departure the Lord changed a few things. Rob was now a member of the Spanish church and didn't seem to be so strong-headed about Bolivia. He invited me out. While enjoying Mexican food on our first date, I did my best to explain WEC's principles and practices regarding engagement and marriage. I thought it was best to explain things clearly right off the bat. He was shocked to learn that, should the relationship continue, he would have to join WEC or I would have to resign. Nevertheless, not long after this, I was introducing him as a potential recruit. I went to Spain and, in the meantime, he applied to WEC.

After a year and a half as a single missionary in Spain, I returned to Canada to be married. Rob still had to finish one more year at Regent College. The Lord gave us the gift of our first daughter, whom we called Karis, 'God's gift'.

Another WEC missionary couple in Vancouver, Frank and Winnie Chapman, had worked in Equatorial Guinea for many years. Missionaries had been expelled from the country by a cruel dictator and were not allowed to return for many years. The Chapmans could see nothing except the need of that small forgotten country, an Hispanic enclave in Central Africa.

Brainwashed

Every time Frank saw us he started to proclaim the same message, 'Equatorial Guinea needs two people who speak Spanish, and who are graduates of Bible College...' Every time we gave the same answer, 'Frank, the Lord must have someone else in mind because we are going to Spain.'

Vancouver is the birthplace of Missions Fest – a very large missionary conference. In 1989 Helen Roseveare was one of the main speakers. She spoke about sacrifice and our willingness to give everything to the Lord. Rob and I left the place that night with the conviction that Spain was no sacrifice for us. We loved the people.

We loved the food. We couldn't wait to get there. But all the way home Frank's 'prophetic' words kept coming to mind. At home we prayed and said that we were willing to make a sacrifice as a real expression of our love for Him.

When we woke up we realized that something would have to be done. The natural steps were to explain to the mission that the Lord was exercising our hearts about sacrifice and maybe He was redirecting us to Equatorial Guinea. However, in those days the mission had no personnel nor any intentions, apart from the Chapmans, to send anyone back to that country. We were told to relax for the time being about Equatorial Guinea. So, feeling that our consciences were clear, we continued with our plans to go back to Spain.

Over refreshments at our farewell service we happened to be seated next to Frank and Winnie Chapman. I noticed that Frank seemed a little nervous. He didn't waste time and soon got to the point. Once again we had to endure the same message about Equatorial Guinea. However, this time there was a different tone. Frank told us his testimony about how the Lord had redirected him from Colombia, even though he already had a Colombian visa which was hard to come by. I could hear Rob attempting to press the fact that we were committed to Spain, the plane tickets could not be refunded, our belongings were sent, etc. Frank had not finished. This time in a more prophetic way he said, 'You think you are going to Spain, but you don't have your visas yet, do you?' If that was a joke, we didn't think much of it. I was glad that we were leaving and wouldn't have to put up with his incessant message any more.

Next day we left for Spain. The first leg of our journey took us to Hamilton, Ontario. The day after, we drove in to Toronto to pick up our passports which we hoped would be stamped with a visa from the Spanish consulate. Our emotions were already loaded after all the farewells so when we found out that our visas had been rejected I couldn't stop crying. I knew the Lord was calling us to Equatorial Guinea.

We immediately sought counsel from Ken and Racile Getty, the Canadian directors of WEC. In this strange game of cat and mouse, once again we were advised to continue heading for Spain. The situation in Equatorial Guinea was still uncertain. There was no team there. Furthermore, we were told, if the Lord should redirect us to this ex-colony of Spain, Madrid was the perfect place to leave from. I felt released, and worse, somehow a little bit proud of ourselves. Like Abraham, the Lord had tested us. We were willing and had said 'yes'. The test was over and we had passed.

Redirected

In Spain on temporary visas, we were so challenged with the many spiritual needs, we forgot all about Equatorial Guinea. As we were looking for an apartment in one of the suburbs of Madrid the leaders of WEC were gathered in Scotland for an International conference. In the back of our minds we remembered that following the conference a group would be meeting in England to seek the Lord's mind about Equatorial Guinea. A group of senior workers from our Spanish field was present at that discussion, and when they returned to Madrid they asked us to meet with them. As soon as they mentioned that the mission had decided to send a team to Equatorial Guinea we knew the Lord wanted us there. Inwardly we said, 'The Lord has called us twice before; this time He won't provide a "scapegoat". We place ourselves on the altar of sacrifice.'

Elliott Tepper who had visited there began to tell us that the country was a mess. The work was very challenging. The living conditions were terribly primitive. However, we would know the Lord's strength and would triumph in the power of Christ. In that instance, I was overcome by fear of death. We knelt on the floor while Billy Glover, Elliott Tepper and Jaap De Bruine laid hands on us. Though I cried and cried, I offered our lives including our daughter as a sacrifice for the sake of the Gospel. The Lord's presence was overwhelming. We had a tremendous sense of joy and afterwards peace triumphed.

Now, as we were going back across the estuary of Rio Muni in the dugout canoe, I recalled the way the Lord led us to this country. His call was so dramatic and empowering. When I compared it with His quiet way of leading us to Spain, I wondered at the difference. I don't think one was right and the other wrong. The distinction was more likely due to the different ministry we would face in Africa. The challenges of life and ministry in Equatorial Guinea were so overwhelming that we needed an unshakeable conviction that this was God's will.

When I look back on our time in Equatorial Guinea I can say that there wasn't one single day in which we didn't thank the Lord for calling us there.

[They have been working with WEC's GATEWAY Cross-cultural Training Centre near Vancouver, BC.]

5

The mills of God grind...quickly!

Sarah* and Robert*

Sarah – Overjoyed to be overseas

Although I come from a non-Christian home, I was fortunate enough to become a Christian at the age of ten. While I don't think I met a missionary in the flesh until I was about twenty, I always had a picture of what being a missionary entailed – a single woman, in some hot and hostile country. (I think I always figured the country was somewhere in Africa.) Accompanying that picture was the fear that God would call *me* to become one. I witnessed friends at university declare their sense of calling to the mission field, but felt no pull in that direction myself, to my great relief. I admired them and I wasn't closed to the idea of God having a plan for me, but I simply wasn't called at that stage.

During my first year after graduation, I was sitting in a Christian meeting, and suddenly became riveted as the speaker read out a request by a missionary in India, for a couple of young people to go and assist with the planning of a speaking tour for J.I. Packer. I couldn't stop thinking about the request – I agonized for about two weeks before I approached the person who had read it out. I worried that because I wanted to go, then surely it couldn't be of God. Yet on the other hand, why would I want to go, if God wasn't putting the desire in my heart? When I finally approached this person I was told that the missionary concerned had decided that a woman wasn't suitable for the job. However, in the meantime, another request had come through for someone to go to Thailand and assist a family working there – primarily by helping with homeschooling their children. I agreed without giving it much further thought, and trusted God to work out the details regarding absence from work, finances, etc., as confirmation of the decision.

To my amazement, I absolutely loved the three-and-a-half months in Thailand. As well as homeschooling, I became involved in a discipleship ministry at an English-speaking campus, picked up a reasonable amount of Thai, and really enjoyed the cultural experience. At the end of my time there, an older missionary couple asked me to consider staying on indefinitely and working in their team. I really wanted to but after much prayer realised I had no peace in my heart about doing so. I sensed I had to go back to New Zealand.

What a change had occurred in me in these nine months! (As well as time in Thailand, I travelled to several other South East Asian countries for experience.) I returned home *very* open to a further and permanent call overseas, although at that stage I wasn't making any active plans. It came as no surprise to me when within a few weeks of arriving back, I met and fell in love with someone with a similar leading...

Robert – Following father's footsteps?

I was born to missionary parents who ultimately spent thirty years of their lives in and around Tokyo. As a consequence, I was able to experience first hand and in a natural manner what it is that missionaries do and the joy that many find in expending themselves in the Lord's work. As well, the missionaries' 'togetherness' and singleminded pursuit of similar goals left a profound impression on my young mind, one that I wouldn't really appreciate until many years after I left Japan, at the age of twelve. When I was about thirteen or fourteen, I went to a Christian camp for young people in New Zealand. Someone prophesied over me during a communion to the effect that I would follow in the footsteps of my parents and that many would come to know Christ as a result. To my young and inexperienced ears, this sounded somewhat fanciful since I had not felt any stirring within my heart, at that point, to walk in my parents' path. A number of years later, I felt a growing restlessness within me to follow the Lord with all my heart. This was accompanied by a strong sense of the need to be holy as the Lord is holy. At an evening church service, when I was twenty-three, I heard a message from Matthew 21 based on the parable of the two sons. The minister concluded his message with a call for the congregation to follow the way of the obedient son who went to work that day in the father's vineyard. I responded to that message by going up to the front of the church, along with about half the congregation, who felt similarly stirred by the Spirit of God. It was a wonderful feeling, as though I was embarking on a new, spiritual adventure.

Over the next few years, I became aware that my occupation would be an excellent entry vehicle for missions because it afforded job opportunities in closed countries. I was also introduced to the book *Operation World* and was overwhelmed by the lack of mission representation in the Arab world. Slowly but surely, God was leading me to the Middle East, specifically the Gulf region.

Sarah – Stirrings within and without

Before we married, we naturally discussed our mutual call overseas. As my own was non-specific, I felt happy to fit in with Robert's pragmatic call to the Gulf, where he could obtain work in any one of about five closed countries. We figured on heading out about five years or so after our marriage, so there didn't seem any real need to do anything hastily with regard to making plans, although in our second year of marriage we enquired as to which New Zealand mission agencies had workers in that area of the world. Much of our thinking then was centred round our imminent transfer to another New Zealand city as part of Robert's work, late the following year. We were looking forward to the change, though aspects of it were unsettling. As we dwelt upon the change, we suddenly did a quantum leap in our thinking. 'If we're going to have to move at the end of next year, why not go overseas instead?' As soon as God had succeeded in getting us to think about His timing instead of our own, the Holy Spirit was really free to work in our lives to guide us specifically. All of a sudden there was a tremendous stirring inside of us and we began to think a lot about going overseas, and specifically, which country of the five the Lord would want us in. We eagerly learned all we could about each. We thought constantly about going – even though at that stage it was at least a year away (we thought!), and, for the first time, we started telling people that we thought God was calling us out. That was in February of 1991.

Throughout February and March, we were deluged with information about one particular Middle Eastern country. Information just seemed to come our way – articles in magazines, a video from a colleague who had worked there, and other contacts from obscure sources.

We continued to pray about the situation, though there seemed no urgency. One Saturday evening as we were talking I finally had the courage to share with Robert that I was sensing that one specific country was the place for us. 'I would have a hard time accepting a job offer from any of the other countries, if they came through,' I said. 'We'll see,' was the pragmatic reply. After all, we had done nothing but get excited about the prospect of going overseas (no job application, no application to a mission society), so it really wasn't worth pursuing the issue. The next day, I spent an extended time in prayer, praying in particular about going to the Middle East. 'Lord,' I said, 'this is a big step we're thinking of taking. If You really want us to go to the Muslims, You're going to have to make it really clear to us that it's Your will.' That was Sunday. Monday afternoon I arrived home from work and was met with the question 'Where do you think I got a telephone call from today?' I gave at least six imaginative replies, before asking to be put out of my misery. It turned out that Robert had been phoned that afternoon and offered a job in the country to which we felt particularly called. If we wanted to take it, we had to be there within twelve weeks!

Robert – A bolt from the blue

After Sarah and I were married, we were inexorably drawn towards the mission field by way of a number of incidents that proved to us that God was directing our steps, even if we didn't know what the ultimate outcome would be. Both of us would read the same articles about the Middle East and be attracted to the region, and in particular, one country. People, when they knew we had a leaning towards mission in the Arab world, would encourage us and give us material to read and mull over. Even our denomination, the Baptist Union, came to the party through their Self Denial Missions programme that highlights a specific area of mission concern every year and targets these needs for prayer and giving. For two successive years, the themes were 'Islam' and 'Tentmaking'. Since we were both on our Mission Committee, we had to do a bit of research of these topics so that we could present the needs to our church effectively. At the same time, our own interest levels were increasing. Finally, the day came when I received the telephone call that Sarah alluded to above, a telephone call that offered me a job in our chosen country immediately.

A gentleman with whom I'd worked in New Zealand, had moved to this country to be the senior professional in my field of work. At this particular time, when we'd felt that God was asking us to go there, he was desperate for recruits and wasn't able to attract the number he needed, so he just started phoning around amongst friends he'd worked with in the past. Of course, he ended up phoning me just at the time that we wanted that final sign of God's leading. Now, this has to be seen in context. We had not sent out any feelers to any part of the Arab world with regard to employment opportunities and we didn't even know that this ex-colleague was in our chosen country. We were planning, as Sarah had indicated, to move to another part of New Zealand with a view to moving overseas perhaps after the end of the year.

The Lord said, 'No. I want you to go today and serve Me in this needy vineyard.' The job offer was like a bolt from the blue. Needless to say, our hearts leapt for joy at such a clear sign of the Lord's direction. We needed no further confirmation about it, or the timetable that we should follow. I immediately resigned from my job and accepted the new appointment. This was followed by a flurry of activity as we approached different mission agencies to see if we could somehow be fast-tracked into their selection process because of the nature and speed of God's call on our lives. We are grateful that we were led to WEC International and that our particular circumstances were met with a flexible and enthusiastic attitude by those responsible.

(Pseudonyms have been used for security reasons)

6

The issue is simple

Nan Pin Chee, Hong Kong

Complete turnaround

Cross-cultural missionary service is not just for
Westerners. God also calls Asians to the mission
field. I am a Chinese, from Malaysia. While I
was studying in New Zealand, God caught me.
He wrought a complete turnaround in my
desires and hopes, so that in the end what I
wanted so dearly in the natural, I didn't really
want at all, and what I came to desire so deeply
was what He wanted for me all along.

My parents are idol worshippers. Although
ancestor worship has existed for many
generations and is part of the fibre of my society,
I did not believe either in this, or in anything
else. But after one year of study in New Zealand,
I became a Christian. That year I was homesick
and lonely. I found the pressures hard and study
difficult. The climate was cold and for the first
time in my life I had to cook my own meals.
I'm a 'science' person and I began asking
questions about life and about the purpose of
my existence. A Christian took me to a
fellowship meeting. Somehow I was touched and
I realized that here was something different. But

61

I didn't know what. I continued to attend because I liked the atmosphere, and in time I pinpointed the different characteristics: they were concern and care. People asked me if I had enough warm clothes, and they invited me home for meals. I enjoyed the companionship and liked to hear the speakers. I thought to myself, 'These Christians really seem to care about people and to have some sort of power in their lives. I want to have that too.' I was not involved in my parents' religion and had no problem about feeling disloyal to their culture. I wanted this new life and the warmth of the Christian fellowship group. I realized Jesus Christ was the Source, and at that point of recognition and faith my life took on meaning and purpose.

Research and renunciation

When I finished my degree, I opted for more grinding study and gained an M.Sc. in Biochemistry. I was involved in research work, and my specialized area concerned the structure of sugar in the brain. In particular, I was researching the effects of this in babies. A baby could die within twelve months if the body did not metabolize sugar. I loved research. It challenged my mind and gave me deep satisfaction when I discovered an answer that was another piece in the jigsaw.

During this time I decided to attend theological college on a part-time basis. I had no lofty ambitions about it, I just wanted to get to know the Bible better. A few thoughts about mission work flashed through my mind during the early days of college, but during my second year, I knew the Lord was speaking to me. People now ask me, 'How did you know?' Deep down inside me I just knew. A question kept on coming back to me: 'What are you going to do with your faith? Are you going to enjoy it by yourself, or are you going to share it?'

Perhaps, because I am a scientist and think in absolutes, I knew that sharing my faith, for me, would be a full-time commitment and that scientific research would have to go. I could not have the two at the same time. Research is doing something that nobody has ever done before. It is looking into the unknown. It is challenging, exciting. In research I knew the techniques and I knew the steps to take along the research path, leading into the unknown. But to share my faith with others, full time, I must step into something new to me. I didn't want to go against God, but I didn't answer His question. It kept nagging at me: 'What are you going to do with your faith? Enjoy it by yourself, or share it?' By not answering I was stalling for time. The issue, simply was: fulltime work for the Lord, or work as a research scientist.

I wrestled over this for nearly two years at theological college and although it appeared to be an issue of vocation, I realized that it was

really a deeper issue. It was a struggle with self.
I had to decide *what* I had to give up for the
Lord and I had to decide *if* I was prepared to
give it up. The sacrifice was the love of my work
– my career.

If there's peace in your heart, keep going

I shared with another student at theological
college that the Lord seemed to be asking me to
go into full-time work and I admitted that I
wanted to keep my full-time job as a research
scientist. I shared also, at that time, some of the
deeper, more personal anxieties I had concerning
the reaction of my family in Malaysia,
concerning financial security and the uncertainty
in my heart. We shared scriptures and always
ended our conversation in prayer. Imagine my
excitement when, during one of these times my
colleague said he was going into full-time
Christian work. Our times of sharing continued
and I was grateful for advice: 'If there is a peace
in your heart, then just keep on going.' I kept
on praying and fasting. Secretly, I was hoping
for some verses of scripture from the Lord.
Nothing came. Looking back, I already knew
the answer. That is why nothing came; God
knew that I already knew.

My struggle continued. I was anxious about
my family's reaction. I thought of their high
hopes for me; they would think I would be
wasting my university education. And what

The issue is simple

about financial and material security? Finally, I wrote them a letter and told them I had become a Christian. They did not know I was studying theology. I did not ask for understanding from them. I simply made a statement, saying I had made up my mind to become a missionary. Their reply took three months and they expressed their reaction in the final sentences. They were disappointed in my decision. Full-time Christian work is dependent on charity. Charity is only for cripples and the socially unfit and 'we don't want one of those in the family' – a traditional Chinese view.

Softly, softly, the desire to feed my intellect with the challenge and power of research, was melted by the Holy Spirit. What God had wrought was a gradual process and what had been so dear, became not so dear at all. I thought of Paul, '...forgetting what lies behind and straining forward to what lies ahead, I press toward the goal for the prize of the upward call of God in Christ Jesus' (Philippians 3:13,14). I remember thinking to myself, 'OK Lord, I'll press forward'.

I thank God that He put across my path an understanding student with whom I could share my doubts. Much encouragement during my lengthy struggle came from these times of sharing together. How marvellous are His ways!

That other student is now my wife.

We know that we are in the centre of God's will. God has given us purpose and fulfilment in the ministry. We have proved that what God says He is, He really is. Jesus said, '...My yoke is easy and my burden is light'. We have found this to be so.

7

National Service – With WEC!

Luc Greiner, France/Senegal

During my studies at an engineering school near Lille, in northern France, I was thinking about the national service issue. In those days, unless one was disabled, which was not my case, every Frenchman had to undertake national service in some form or other: one year of military service, or two years civil service (only for those who had been recognized by the government as conscientious objectors, and that was quite difficult), or sixteen months of voluntary service somewhere overseas (for example, being a teacher or a doctor or a development projects helper, mainly in former French colonies). I was thinking and praying about the last possibility.

The university I attended was far away from home: I knew hardly anybody, except the ten members of the tiny little church I attended.

We had our Christmas celebration, and quite a number of people from other small churches in the Lille area joined us for that day. It was the first time I had met most of them, so our pastor introduced me to some. One of them was

Martin, from Alsace, where I too came from. He greeted me in an unusual way: he went straight into asking me questions. 'Have you already done your national service?' 'No, I have not.' 'Do you know that there is a possibility of voluntary service overseas *with Christian missions or churches?*' 'No, I haven't heard about that last bit.' So Martin started to explain that arrangement to me.

Well, that unusual encounter seemed to me to be a hint from the Lord, and it did not take me long to come to the conclusion that, because I had to serve my country anyway, it would be best to serve the Lord at the same time. So I started looking around for an opportunity. Martin had warned me: the French government had delegated the recruitment of volunteers for Christian service to a catholic non-governmental organization for those who were Catholics, and to the Département Evangélique Français d'Action Apostolique; a branch of the former Mission Evangélique de Paris for all the rest, ranging right through from the most liberal Protestants to the most extreme Pentecostals. Therefore, Martin said, I should look for work with a mission that has a theological orientation I could share, rather than taking the risk of having to work in a setting where, perhaps there would not be any Christian faith at all. He himself had done things this way.

I wrote to many Christian organisations and missions, but those who answered just told me 'get in touch with the DEFAP'.

I didn't know what to do.

But then, I happened to be back in my home church, and one Sunday we had a visit from an elder of a sister church in Switzerland. Somebody told me: 'This man is involved in missions. May be you should tell him about your problem.' So I did. He said he would see what he could do for me. I didn't even know which mission he was working with.

A few weeks later, I received a letter from WEC in Switzerland telling me that they had a positive answer from WEC in Senegal and that there was a possibility of me working among young people in Ziguinchor. Alleluia! (If I remember properly, it was the first time I had heard about WEC!)

I saw this as the door the Lord had opened for me, and so I wrote to the DEFAP, to tell them that I would like to work with WEC as a youth worker in Ziguinchor, Senegal, and to ask for an official application form. I also wrote to WEC to ask them to tell the DEFAP that they needed a youth worker and that they would like to have me. Exactly the way Martin had told me to proceed.

Well, the answer from the DEFAP was not very nice. I just remember the first sentence, 'Dear sir, we inform you that it is *we* who decide where you will go and *not you!*' Not easy, this first contact with them!

I said to the Lord, 'This man is wrong: it is not he who decides, but You, Lord'. Still, the relation with the DEFAP was a bit difficult.

Before sending an application form, they wanted to interview me first. So, over the next seven months they set up different appointments, but cancelled most of them at the last minute. Time was getting short. I had only six months left before I would have to go to the army, if no proper arrangement was made with DEFAP.

I went on praying about this. Finally, they proposed another appointment for the very next day, in a town 500 km from Lille! I got permission for time off from university, travelled all night by train, and was there in time for the appointment. The interview was very formal, but went well, and finally I got the needed official application form.

This was the 28th January. The deadline for the completed form to be back at the DEFAP was fixed at February 15th!

Most documents they asked for were quite easy to obtain, but one was a medical certificate from the Army, telling that I was medically fit to serve overseas. Like every Frenchman, when I was 18, I had already spent three days in an army centre, where they checked my fitness for military service, and I had then received a document with the feared words 'medically fit' (feared because they meant I couldn't escape national service). But for us who wanted to go overseas, we needed to pass a second exam at the army medical centre, in order to get a second certificate with the same, but this time desired, words 'medically fit' (desired because this meant that at least you could escape military service).

Several other fellow students had filled in the same forms (but to go on secular work), and in order to get this medical certificate, they had written to the army and asked for an interview with a doctor, and waited three long months just to get *an appointment*. I needed THE RESULT of the medical check within two weeks! It seemed impossible, but I was confident and said to the Lord that I knew, if it was His will, He would do a miracle.

I wrote on 28th January to ask for an appointment. On 11th February, I got the answer: not the desired appointment with the army doctor, but the final document telling that I was medically fit! Without a second visit! The miracle had happened! I had all the required documents in time! Alleluia!

Well, then came the less exciting time of waiting for the official answer. Would my request be accepted? 'Lord, it is in Your hands!' I waited, and I prayed.

I had been told that if a pastor would contact the DEFAP and back up my request, this would help. But I had decided not to ask anybody to do that. No! I wanted the Lord to act.

Soon after that there was a missionary conference organized in Lille. Important speakers like Patrick Johnstone had been invited. I attended several meetings. A missionary exhibition had also been organized, with many missions having a display. Even the DEFAP had a stand. I avoided the temptation to spend time at it trying to manipulate a favourable reply.

The congress came to an end. We were on our way back to the car when a pastor who knew about my application caught up with me, followed by the man who was on the DEFAP stand. Before I could say a word, this pastor started to explain to the other man that I wanted to serve overseas and that I had filled in an application form with the DEFAP, etc. The man said he would phone to Paris and try to get my dossier through.

I was shattered. 'Oh no, Lord! That is exactly what I did not want to happen!'

Two days later I received the final answer: I was accepted as a youth worker with WEC in Senegal. I then checked the date on the stamp. The letter had been posted two days *before* the conference! So it was the *Lord's* working, not men's intervening.

I graduated from engineering school in June and went to Senegal in September, to serve the Lord for two years, instead of serving in the

French army. It was a great time, spending hours in the reading room talking to students who were eager to know about Jesus, running youth camps, showing the Jesus film, and speaking at many youth meetings.

But at the same time I was burdened by the question every short-termer asks himself: 'What will I do after these two years?' I started to pray earnestly about it, but got no answer for a while. Then, one morning, during my prayer time, it was as if the Lord said to me, 'Why do you ask Me what you should do after these two years? Why don't you think about what you could do?'

Well, actually, it was not easy to do that. I started with the main possibilities: looking for work according to my qualifications, or switching to full-time service for the Lord. Then I stopped. These two were quite acceptable options to me at that time. But I felt there was a third one: to get further training. And I didn't want to write that one down on my notes. Did I not say to my friend André the very day we both graduated, 'André, I have spent twenty years of my life at school. Today was *the* last!' And now I had this impression that the Lord asked me just to be willing to look into this possibility again.

It was a struggle for many days, maybe weeks. But finally I gave in to the Lord and noted that possibility. I noted it down with two sub-headings: 'Pursue more training in professional skills' and 'Head for Bible training'. That last one again was a struggle: I come from an evangelical family, and had had lots and lots of good teaching. My knowledge about the Bible was quite high, so why go to Bible school? That's for people who did not have a proper Christian teaching during childhood. But I had to note it down.

Then I started to obtain as much information as possible on these points. I wrote to universities, wrote for information about work opportunities, and wrote to Bible schools.

But the Lord's answer came in a different way.

One day, our field leaders, Bob and Sue Pritchard, asked me if I could translate WEC's English leaflet on Senegal into French. I tried. But translating a leaflet is one of the most difficult things I know, because the text is so condensed and every single word is so loaded with meaning. If you don't know the background, you will surely mis-translate. So I went back to Bob and Sue and asked them to give me all the documentation that had been used to produce the English leaflet. They gave me many kilos of paper, and I started to read them.

I then came across a survey on Senegal written by Jonathan McRostie from OM. I had read this survey already twice before, once during my orientation at the WEC headquarters in Switzerland and once during my orientation on the field.

But while reading it for the third time, suddenly I was struck by one sentence: 'People group: Soninké; size of the group: 386,000; religion: 70% Muslim, 30% Animist; scripture translation: nothing, but needed; number of believers/churches: none known'. When I finished reading that line I said to the Lord, 'Lord, if this is where you want to send me, I am ready'. And immediately I knew this was where He wanted me. I knew I would have to go to Bible school (compulsory before applying to most missions), but this was no longer a problem. The Lord had spoken and my heart was changed.

I went to Bible school (and enjoyed it, learning a lot); I got married; we went to the Senegal field, and after a first four-year term working with a team among the Fulas, we finally started to learn the Soninké language. Alleluia!

8

A fall on the stairs cured my depression

Shin Chul Lee, Korea/Ghana

Recently I had a phone call 'out of the blue' from America. It was from Woo Young Choi, who led me to the Lord through one-to-one Bible study when I was a student at university. He is now a chaplain in the US Army, and I am a missionary to the Dagomba people in Ghana.

Two great homes

Before I met Mr Choi, I had already been blessed through my two Christian homes. My father's uncle was a deeply devoted pastor in whose house I stayed nine-and-a-half years while my father was studying abroad. After the first seven years my mother went abroad to be with him. I was left with my father's uncle. That's why I call him and auntie 'Grandpa' and 'Grandma'. They have already gone to be with the Lord but I miss them very much. They loved me and showed me an example of the real Christian life. My parents came back when I was ten. I joined them and had my second Christian home. I was really blessed through that too. I grew up with their balanced love and teaching. I don't think I could have had a better home. I was active in the youth group at church and I used to take part in the prayer meetings and felt happy in Jesus. But when I became sixteen years of age I began to be doubtful about God and His existence. I found myself falling into sinful ways. My family knew about it and prayed for me day and night. It took quite some years before I repented and received Jesus as my Lord through Mr Choi's influence and teaching.

While at university, I became actively involved in witnessing to the students. It was such a joy for me to see one accept Jesus as Lord that I told the Lord I wanted to be a missionary and would go wherever He sent me. After graduation, I was admitted to the Kosin Theological Seminary where my father taught. In the first year, I experienced spiritual depression. I realized how weak I was on my own. I saw so many failures and contradictions in me. I cried to the Lord, 'O Lord, I am not worthy to be a missionary.' But the answer of the Lord was so amazing. 'It's not you, but I, who called you to be a missionary.' At that moment, I knelt down on the floor and committed myself to the Lord again. Since then I have had great joy and peace whenever I think of my missionary calling.

At the end of the first year in seminary, the Lord gave me a wonderful gift – my wife. She was quite sure that the Lord called her to be a partner of a full-time minister but was unsure that she could be a missionary wife. It took some time for her to become certain of her calling. She went to a mission conference and gave up her own idea about the future and gave her life to the Lord. She was really moved by the fact that Jesus our Lord left the glory of heaven and became a man like ourselves. She felt that Jesus was the first missionary in the world. I thanked the Lord for His gentle touch on her life.

Under pressure

During the first few years of our marriage I was under pressure. I had two roles, as a youth worker and as an assistant to the pastor of the church. I was still a student at the seminary and just recently married. Life was not easy. My wife had a baby and that brought extra responsibilities. I still wish I could have done better than I did. I was not strong in Greek and Hebrew. The youth group was growing and encouraging me but my occasional sermons to the congregation were not impressive. It was not easy to be a good husband and I felt depressed. But our Lord was so good. He intervened in a special way.

One morning, I was stepping down the outdoor stairs holding our little daughter in my arms, I slipped and my head hit a big clay pot at the foot of the flight. The pot broke and cut my right cheek and ear. It could have been a fatal wound, but the Lord saved my life. After a long operation the torn parts of the face and ear were stitched to the right places. By God's grace Eun Jin, our daughter, had not been hurt at all. At that time I realized that the Lord was dealing with me through the incident. I had a fresh sense of His love. The accident did not have a negative effect on me at all. Rather it helped me to wake up from my spiritual depression. I then had to have a break for one year but was able to have more quiet times with the Lord. I resumed my study the next year and completed the seminary course.

My wife and I were eager to train for missionary work and to improve our English, but in Korea we could not find a suitable missionary training course. Suddenly we were reminded of the book, *Operation World*, from which we used to get some information about mission fields. We found the WEC address in Britain and also contacted Rev. Buk-kyung Kim, a Korean pastor in London. Through him we were introduced to Dr David Burnett, the principal of the Missionary Orientation Centre. With his invitation letter, we were able to get visas for Britain.

God undertook for us in the UK. We enrolled at the MOC and when our money ran low He provided a scholarship through the Korean Church in Kingston. Language was another obstacle for us. We felt so helpless with very limited English. We were sure that we were experiencing culture shock in Britain, even before we got to the mission field. As we prayed, however, God moulded us. We became interested in Ghana, because we heard that the Ghanaian government did not welcome any new missionaries unless a mission or a church in Ghana invited them using its missionary quota.

Encouraged by WECers

That is how we began to think of joining WEC. Howard and Gill Sayers, then candidate secretaries, were very kind and introduced us to Graham and Marj Bee, the field leaders of WEC, Ghana. The initial responses from them were encouraging. To go further, we had to go back to Korea and be sent by the church there. At that time the churches in our denomination sent missionaries through the mission board. When we shared our burden for the Muslims in Ghana they were excited to hear this and introduced us to the Women's Association of the denomination, as a supporting body. This is a group of highly organized housewives eager to pray for and support missionaries. We were very happy to get their prayerful support. The mission board agreed to the idea of our joining WEC in Ghana for two reasons: the mission board could not care for us in the mission field effectively, and it did not have the proper channels to send us there.

So after completing the candidate course we joined WEC. It was flexible enough to welcome a Presbyterian couple and vice versa. We liked WEC's interdenominational stand without losing its Biblical standard. We liked the WEC leadership style in the field and in the sending bases. We also liked WEC's commitment to unreached peoples and its openness to internationalization.

We worked among the Dagomba people, the largest Muslim people group in the country, for a number of years and more recently have been appointed WEC representatives in Tak Jeon, Korea.

9

From Islam, Communism and Capitalism to Christ

Ali Khan* and Anna*

Ali's story
'Good boy'

I was brought up in a Muslim country, according to Islam's traditions. In my childhood I sincerely tried to accomplish the required rituals and duties. I used to get up early in the morning to pray. Daily I tried to do such good deeds as I could, like helping elderly people and being obedient to parents and relatives. As children, we were encouraged to keep increasing our good deeds to gain salvation. In fact, the Muslims believe that each person has two angel-scribes: one on his right shoulder writing down good deeds, the other on his left shoulder noting the bad ones.

Frankly, I struggled with this concept for several years till one day, when I became a teenager, I had the courage to ask myself, 'Is this the only way of salvation in the world?' This lack of assurance led me to have doubts about Allah and his existence.

False freedom

Philosophers like Jean-Paul Sartre had a powerful influence on youngsters like myself. Existentialism had a tremendous impact on us. I felt released from the fear of hell and found a way to escape the judgment of Allah. Atheism gave me a new sense of identity, but it did not last for long. It was like the short-lived joy given to shipwrecked people on a desert island when a boat appears on the horizon and then disappears before they can be rescued.

I left my country and went to live in Europe.

In Belgium, where I stayed for about six years, I deserted capitalism. While I worked in different places, I became involved with a group of communist activists. I liked their concern for social issues and the help they offered to foreigners. I enjoyed their company, friendship and enthusiasm.

'The Camarades' as we called each other, persuaded me to go for a high degree in a communist country. The entry visa to the former USSR was complicated and I was not keen to follow the difficult procedure to get it. I opted to go to another country in the Eastern block instead. 'The Camarades' were very supportive during my first year of language study, but communism in the West, I learned later, is like the tip of an iceberg. We discovered its true stature only when we moved into the 'cold waters' of the Eastern block.

The first witness

During the years I spent in this socialist country, I learnt that all the things my 'camarades' dreamed of in the West about communism were rubbish. People were more self-centred and immoral. But during my stay in the student residential blocks at the university I noticed the behaviour of two students: one was from Lebanon, the other was from Syria. Both of them were kind, loving and caring. Both were Christians.

During my studies I continued my militant activities within the student body, which was apolitical and recognized by the governing party. The last four years of my involvement with the young communists gave me an understanding of the heart of the system. It consisted of atheism, selfishness, corruption, immorality and pride.

The year before my course ended I visited my home country to see how things were in the world of medicine. I was appalled by the corruption and the money-grabbing attitude of many doctors. When I returned to the country where I studied for my final year, I was still searching for answers to life's problems. After graduation I felt I needed a year to reflect and consider my future so I took a further year of study in Britain to learn English.

I was walking along Edgeware Road in London when a dark-skinned person, working with Operation Mobilization approached me and handed a leaflet to me. It was the testimony of four people, telling what Christ had done in their lives. I was impressed by it, but even more importantly, I was reminded of the two Christians that I met during my studies. Now I had the clue as to why they were so different from the others! A few weeks later I accepted Jesus Christ as my Saviour and Lord in a small church in London.

The vision
After that year I worked with OM in its *Love Europe* programme, reaching out to Muslims visiting London. John, the director of this ministry, was very concerned afterwards to find a place for me in a Christian organisation running a medical project. The vision was also shared with the small church where I had become a Christian. Several people were involved in earnest prayer and support. One day John phoned me to inform me about a mission called WEC International which was looking urgently for doctors. We are now serving the Lord overseas.

Just Dreams?
by Anna*

Direction or Imagination?

'Come with me to Maikura*!' Deliah*, a woman I worked with, was speaking to me in a dream. Where was Maikura? I looked it up in an atlas and found it. Was God telling me to leave the business of my parents behind in Europe and go to this far off region which I knew nothing about?

During the space of about one month I had three dreams which pointed me towards changing the direction of my life, towards forgetting the option of having a 'normal' life in my home country and towards going to Maikura. Was this really the Lord's will or just my imagination?

I was glad to be able to go to a camp where people who were interested in missions could get more information. On the first evening a leader of WEC spoke about the many possibilities there were for persons working in their profession, being at the same time missionaries. He explained also that there was a great need for such 'tent-makers' in so-called 'closed countries' where open evangelism is prohibited or impossible. On the same evening I spoke with him about my dream and asked if WEC had work in Maikura. From the nature of his reply I assumed (wrongly) that it had no workers there.

Fishing around

After talks with missionaries and friends I wrote letters to different missions. I got some answers, but nobody seemed to have a team in the region of Maikura. Then I was invited to attend the conference of a mission which worked in neighbouring regions. A missionary shared that she had known for a long time that God wanted her to go to Dargya*. Many obstacles were in her way and the visa was refused several times, but the Lord took her in and she stayed for over twenty years. She added that the team had had many external and internal struggles and that she was able to stay on only because she knew that the Lord had placed her there. The leader of the mission told me that I could work with them in any one of the several regions. But I still had this question: Did the Lord not want me to go to Maikura itself? Was it right to join a team just because it was in a nearby region?

Shortly afterwards I visited another mission. I learned about their plans and projects, but I would have needed to learn two different languages and neither of those was the language spoken in Maikura. When I drove home praying, all of a sudden a chapter of Scripture came to my mind. I looked it up and found to my astonishment that Maikura was mentioned there. I had not realised this before. I shared the whole story with good friends, whom I saw once a week for Bible study and prayer. After I had finished someone said, 'You cannot go there just because of these dreams and this chapter. That is just not enough.' I answered that I wanted to go only if I was 100 per cent sure that this was God's will, especially as it affected my parents and their business.

The morning after this talk, before I started reading my Bible, I told the Lord: 'If Maikura is mentioned, not in a dream or a Bible verse, but from a source outside of me, which I cannot control or influence, then I will take it that You want me to go there'. And what happened? My book of daily devotions for that same day mentioned this country. And the Sunday afterwards our pastor preached about inhabitants of Maikura. From then on I was certain that God wanted me to go there, but I still did not know of any organization working in it.

The net closes

A few days later I visited a mission which had been working previously in Maikura. When I told them my story and my certainty that I should work there, they phoned Frances, a missionary who had been working there. She informed me about two organizations which worked there. One of them was WEC. The other mission was from Gordes*, a country with a culture and language different from my home country. This mission did not have a base nearby. WEC, on the other hand, was known to me through the biography of C.T. Studd by Norman Grubb, and the contact from the camp. Also, it had a centre nearby. It was clear to me that WEC was the organization I should seek to join. I immediately wrote to them.

That evening when I came home after having met Frances, I told my parents about my change of plans and how it had come clear to me that I should not continue in their business but live and work in Maikura. They had been suspecting something for several months, but I had not wanted to tell them anything before I was sure of the right decision. I had not wanted to involve them in the uncertainty of the past six months. It was difficult for them to adjust to the sudden change. But they have a strong faith and understood my guidance. I explained to them also, that in any case I could never guarantee to continue in the business forever. My parents and my whole family have been very supportive until now and I am very grateful for that.

Some days after the talk with Frances, my parents and I had the opportunity to watch slides and hear about Maikura at an evening organized by one of my friends who had visited the region. About two years later I started working in Maikura with WEC and that's where Ali* and I met.

*Names have been changed for security reasons.

10

It all started in a beauty salon

Anna Clarke, Taiwan/Guinea Bissau

I thought Jesus was an American God

I was born in a small village on the east coast of Taiwan. There were no churches or Christians. The traditional beliefs of the village people were Buddhism and Ancestor Worship. My father at that time painted Buddhas on the glass part of altars used in most homes. I never heard about Jesus during my childhood. When I left school, I began working in a beauty salon – where I met Jesus.

The Lord sent a single lady from Chicago to Mongolia to work as a missionary with TEAM (The Evangelical Alliance Mission). When forced to leave, Angie went to the east coast of Taiwan and came to the beauty salon once a month. She used to read something while waiting and she told me that Jesus had died for me. I laughed in my heart, thinking that Jesus was an American god. At that time life was meaningless and my heart was empty, but I didn't want Jesus. One day a colleague suggested to me that we visit Angie. We had been invited many times and although we said we would visit, we hadn't. We went, and had some American biscuits and Chinese tea. I felt that she was very happy, but I didn't understand why. Something attracted me to her. Some time before that she had given me a Chinese New Testament, but I didn't want it and threw it away. Now, I wanted to know the truth. Eventually Angie began studying the Bible with me, nearly every day for about four months.

One day I was sitting alone upstairs in the staff room of the salon, reading my Bible. In the room were eight Buddhas sitting on a shelf. Suddenly, I realized that the Buddhas weren't real and that Jesus died for me and I needed Him. I cried out to Him asking Him to forgive me and I received Him as my Saviour. I was so happy! I told all the customers that I was a Christian. They told me I was crazy and that I was following an American god.

A problem with food

My family at that time, like most Taiwanese families, offered all their food to Buddha and the family ancestor before eating. I could not eat anything because all the food had been offered to idols. After some time, my mum started to keep some food for me before it was offered to the ancestors and Buddha.

Six months after I came to Jesus I was baptized. My parents were very unhappy. Mum said that

I wasn't part of the family. I found it very difficult having to choose between Jesus and them, because I loved both. Many times I was not allowed to go to church. It seemed that the whole family was against me. However I took one younger brother to a church camp where he met the Lord, and another younger brother to an evangelistic meeting where he was converted. My parents, older brother and sister all gave them a very difficult time but one of these brothers later became a pastor. After that, my parents started to notice that we were better children than before.

In the salon I had to work seven days a week. I did not want to work on Sundays, and so gave up this job and moved to Taipei where I began work in a Christian orphanage of TEAM and attended a TEAM church. During my time there I committed myself to full-time service for the Lord. I was very challenged by the message from Esther 4:14, 'For if you remain silent at this time, relief and deliverance for the Jews will arise from another place, but you and your father's family will perish.' I took this to heart and took it to mean 'If you do not speak about Jesus to others, your people will be lost and perish'. I was very touched by this. Soon after hearing this, I was wakened at 3am by the lady with whom I shared a room. 'Why are you crying?' she asked me. 'I'm not,' I replied, but when I touched my face, I was. I went into another room and read my

Bible. I remember thinking about seeing thousands of people all calling out, 'Save me, save me!' If I didn't tell them about Jesus, they would all perish. That was why I was crying. I read Isaiah 6:8, committed myself to the Lord, and decided that I should go to Bible college and serve Him full-time.

Don't send me, send my colleague

I went to the OMS (Oriental Missionary Society) Theological College and during my second year at a student retreat, a Chinese pastor working in Brazil talked about mission. He asked, 'Why are all the missionaries westerners? Why are there no Chinese missionaries? What do Chinese people do? They open restaurants and satisfy people's stomachs; they want money.' He asked, 'Are God's commands only for foreigners and not for Chinese?' 'As the Father has sent me, so I am sending you.' I thought only Chinese people needed the Gospel. I hadn't thought about other peoples. I felt that I didn't have the ability to learn another language, so I prayed, 'Lord, don't send me, send my colleague'. Later I went back to my room and felt the Lord reminding me that I belonged to Him and that He wanted me. I promised the Lord that wherever He wanted me to go, I would go. At that time I had no idea where that would be.

While studying at College, I taught Sunday school. One day I was telling the children a story

about a small African boy who became a
Christian, and challenged them to pray for the
children of Africa. At that time I didn't know
much about that place, but I sensed the Lord
prompting me, 'Why don't you go to Africa?' I
thought, 'How can I go? I don't know much
about it.' Later, God gave me a heavy burden
for that continent, even though I knew little
about it. From then on, I told my colleagues
and teachers at the College that I was going to
Africa to preach the Gospel. Some people said
it was too far, others said it was impossible. They
thought I was crazy. Usually Taiwanese went
to America, but not Africa.

I graduated from College still with a vision
for Africa in my heart. I worked in Taiwan
planting churches for four years with
missionaries from TEAM. At that time, they
were sending missionaries only from America,
not Taiwan. One day I visited a former colleague
from OMS and she asked me why I wasn't in
Africa. I replied that I didn't know how to get
there and that I was satisfied serving the Lord in
Taiwan, speaking Chinese, and living with my
family. This lady gave me a Chinese copy of the
Look magazine (from WEC). I had never seen
one before and that happened to be the last issue
in Chinese. It had a lot of information about
West Africa in it and Guinea-Bissau attracted
me, although I knew nothing about it. On the
last page was an offer for anyone interested in

mission work to contact Doug Plummer, who was at that time the WEC field leader in Taiwan.

Mum didn't want me in Africa

Doug Plummer said that if the Lord had called me to Guinea-Bissau, I would have to learn English, Portuguese, and an African language. It all seemed to be too difficult. I wondered how I could ever get there. But I started to trust the Lord for His guidance and His supply. I had peace from the Lord. Gene McBride (then field leader of Guinea-Bissau) wrote to me and told me about many difficulties in the country. At that time, the country didn't have enough food to feed the people. They had some rice and sweet potatoes but meat, vegetables, milk and other basic foods were very difficult to obtain. Missionaries had to bring their own tinned food with them, enough for three or four years! I couldn't understand this situation and wondered what this place must be like. A verse came to mind – 'The Good News is preached to the poor' (Luke 7:22). I told the Lord that the poor people in this place needed Jesus and that I was willing to go. Mum didn't want me to go but God did. It was difficult to leave my family, but I had peace.

Before I left Taiwan, I had an opportunity to marry a pastor who was a classmate and I had to choose: either a husband and church work in Taiwan, or obey God's call to go to Africa as a missionary. The Lord gave me victory. I thought I would never get married because there were no single Chinese men missionaries going to Africa. But I was happy to be single and serve the Lord there.

I did my candidate course in Bulstrode in England during 1983. I noticed that the International Secretary, Stewart Dinnen, and other people in high positions took turns at washing the dishes and other practical duties. This was the opposite to my culture. I was impressed very much and felt that WEC was a down-to-earth mission with a simple sacrificial lifestyle. This attracted me very much. I felt part of the WEC family.

When I arrived in Guinea-Bissau the first time, it was 2am; there was only one flight each week. At the airport building everything was very dark and the customs people checked all my luggage with a torch. I was very excited to be in Africa because the Lord wanted me to be there. I was too excited to sleep that first night. Early the next morning, I heard many voices talking outside the mission headquarters. I opened the window and saw many ladies carrying baskets on their heads. People were coming and going and somehow I felt that the whole society was quite strange. Everyone was black; I had never seen so many black people before. However, I found that the Africans were very friendly, especially the Christians; they gave me a lovely welcome. African society is very family oriented, just like the Chinese.

I had to learn how to fit in with the African way of life, such as no timetable, no schedule, visiting any time. One thing that helped me is that Africans like to talk, and I like to talk too!

Shocks to the system

I had culture shock. Next door to the mission headquarters was a public drinking place where people drank cashew wine and men urinated against our wall. The smell was bad and I found it hard to adapt. Another thing: Africans have bathrooms outside their homes with a low fence around them. When you walk past, they call out to you and want to have a conversation while they are having a shower! For them, it is natural, but for me it was very difficult.

Working with a multinational team was also difficult at first. In Taiwan I had been teaching American missionaries to speak Chinese and had been church planting with them too. When I took the candidate course and studied English in Britain I got to know other nationalities and their ways of thinking. This helped me when I arrived on the field. I learned to accept the many different ways of thinking. On the field, I found it difficult because I had to speak to the other missionaries in English. I also had to learn Creole. Most of the WECers on the field had never been to Asia and didn't understand

Chinese thinking. Perhaps they saw me as strange. For this reason I tried to open up and communicate with them. I felt accepted by the others and we worked well together as a team. I didn't have any difficulty in making friends with either Africans or co-workers.

After my first term of service I went home, and that was when my mum came to the Lord while in hospital. I was so excited! Then I did extra studies at the WEC Missionary Training College in Tasmania. I wasn't interested in any of the students, but the Lord called one of them, Kevin Clarke, to WEC and to the unreached peoples of Guinea-Bissau. Then God brought us together. I never thought about marrying anyone from another culture but the Lord widened my point of view! Because we are from different backgrounds, we talk a lot and listen a lot to each other so that we can understand each other. We are very happy to be serving the Lord here in Guinea Bassau.

Family following my faith footsteps

My mother died four months after our wedding in Taipei. I had always been very close to her and found her death very hard to accept. My father was saved and died sixteen days after mum. We stayed in Taiwan for eight months and then left for Portugal so that Kevin could learn Portuguese. We knew that the Lord's timing for everything was perfect. A month later another young member of my family, a niece, came to the Lord; we were praising the Lord for that! I believe that all of my family will be saved eventually. With God all things are possible.

11

List your faith targets

Ian and Dianne Cash, Côte d'Ivoire

Already involved

My wife, Dianne, and I had been married for
thirteen years. In that time we had purchased a
house, car, and all the trappings, and had been
blessed with a boy and a girl who were nearing
the end of their primary schooling and
developing musical talents with great success. I
had been teaching for eighteen years, mainly
with the lower primary grades, in which I found
much fulfilment. Dianne was using her
secretarial and book-keeping skills in the church
and local state school on a part-time basis. Both
of us were committed to serving the Lord
amongst the children of our church, and I was
involved in the primary ISCF work in
Queensland, chairing the state committee and
directing holiday camps, as well as running a
group at the school where I was teaching.

Our church had begun to move in renewal,
and the Lord had been giving our church
fellowship many promises regarding a future
expansion of the work beyond its present small

numbers. We were excited to sense the hand of the Lord and were seeking Him as to the part He would have us play in this.

However, at the same time, I was feeling an increasing tension at school with continual pressure from children and parents alike to lower my standard of discipline and to compromise my Christian testimony. As the weeks went by I was becoming more and more discouraged and wondered where it was all leading.

During this time, we had read about an urgent need for a primary teacher for the lower grades at Vavoua International School in Côte d'Ivoire. We had known about the school for several years, as Dianne's brother was a WEC missionary there and a member of the school committee. He had suggested several times that we could teach at the school, but we felt the Lord wanted us to remain where we were.

A faith shopping list

However, on Friday 4 November 1984, after a particularly difficult day at school, the Lord caused Dianne to ask me if I felt that the Lord was prompting us to go to Vavoua through the problems I was encountering. So we took pencil and paper and listed the things that would have to happen for us to be sure this move could be of the Lord. Believing that we would go as short term workers for two or three years, our list read something like this:

1. Approval from WEC International, who run the school.

2. Someone to rent the house while we were away.

3. A buyer for our car.

4. Money for the fares to and from Côte d'Ivoire.

5. Support for us while we were at Vavoua.

6. Direction as to whether I should resign or seek leave from the Education Department.

7. Provision for our parents who would have no children at home to care for them.

The very next day at a regular Bible study, we were reading Numbers 13, and the pastor challenged any of us who were thinking of stepping out in a new venture with the Lord to move ahead in faith as Joshua and Caleb were urging the Israelites to do. Our family devotional book also featured the same story, urging us to rise up in faith to accept any new challenges our family was facing. We talked about it as a family, and the children agreed to go, even though it meant delaying their musical studies and leaving good friends.

This encouraged us to talk to our parents about going to Vavoua to fill the need. When we did, both Dianne's Mum and Dad and my widowed mother said they were not surprised because every time they had prayed about the school's need, the Lord had brought us to mind.

They all encouraged us to press on, and not to worry about them as they believed the Lord would care for them if we went. Likewise, when we shared it with our pastor he was very encouraging, although in the natural realm, he would have liked us to stay on in the church.

How the rest all came together

The Lord highlighted Exodus 14:14 from our *Daily Bread* reading – 'The Lord will fight for you, you have only to be still'. So we agreed to rest in the Lord and see what He would do. In the next five weeks, the Lord did fight for us!

1. A couple from Sydney rang us to say that they would help to support us financially while we were at the school and also gave us a large gift towards our air fare.

2. The field workers in Côte d'Ivoire agreed to our coming.

3. An older couple with a teenage son from our church fellowship needed a place to rent, and were happy to rent our home for as long as we were at Vavoua.

4. Our outward fare to Côte d'Ivoire was supplied through many Christians.

Gluttons for more

When we fulfilled our two-year commitment at Vavoua we felt the Lord's leading to stay on for another two years. We finally came home in August, 1989.

Some months later, my wife found employment as the secretary at the Bible College of Queensland and I obtained a teaching position at a Christian school. We were both enjoying the opportunity to minister for the Lord in these ways. Our children completed their university studies and also found employment – our son as an accountant and our daughter as a research assistant. However, at the end of 1993, the Christian school closed for financial reasons, and I was not able to find a permanent position with any other school. I took over the children's work at our church and taught classes in State schools on a relief basis for the next three years.

Because of our continuing interest in the Vavoua International School, we felt that we should ask the Lord to show us if He wanted us to return there, as no job opportunities were opening. However, the Lord showed us that it was not His time for us to make such a move. But several things occurred early in 1996 which seemed to indicate that the Lord might want us to move out of our 'comfort zone'.

1. A house-parent couple at VIS wrote to us, asking us to pray about returning there to fill the position of principal for two years from mid-1997 until the arrival of the next permanent principal.

2. A real estate agent rang, asking if we had thought about selling our house as he had a buyer who wanted to live in our street.

3. While having tea with WEC's Australian directors during their visit to Brisbane in February, they asked if our 'home leave' was over, and we discussed with them what would be required of us by WEC Australia if we were to return to Africa.

4. While reflecting later on what they had said, my wife made the comment that we would have to receive an 'official' invitation from the VIS committee before she would seriously consider going back.

5. Several days later we received such a letter asking me to act as interim principal for two years to fill the gap between two long-term principals.

Thus, we saw that God wanted us to be serious about seeking His will about returning to VIS. So we prayed and waited on God to show us what He required of us. For about a month, it seemed as though He was silent, but at the end of March He spoke to me through my quiet time readings in Ezekiel 2:9-3:21, and 24:15-27.

Family reaction

When we shared what God was saying with our now adult children, they both were very excited and pleased for us, although naturally a little apprehensive about the changes in their circumstances. Similarly, our mothers, who were both widows, were very supportive when we first mentioned it to them. (Both of them have since told us how the Lord had been encouraging them and telling them that He would care for them in our absence.)

We then talked to WEC's Queensland directors, sharing with them how the Lord had been leading us. They told us that they were thrilled to hear our news and that we should write back to VIS.

We did so, stating that we believed that God was asking us to return to VIS. We asked for some further details as to what my job description would be, and what role my wife would have, her preference being for a similar secretarial role to that which she performed during our last term.

We received a short note from the field leader, saying that the field were thrilled to hear that we were willing to return and they were happy for us to come as full-term missionaries. The VIS leaders also sent us a letter, saying that they were thrilled to read of our willingness to accept their invitation, especially on a long-term basis as this would allow continuity of leadership. They felt that my wife would be able to do secretarial duties as before, and maybe assist with the field finances.

Once again the Lord provided for us in every way and we are now back at VIS, feeling very much 'at home' and looking to the Lord to equip us in every way for the task to which He has called us.

[Ian is currently Principal of the Vavoua International School.]

12

The Word, the witness and the weight of circumstances

Christel Meyer, Thailand/Germany

Escape from fire

'What on earth is going on in front of my lab-door?' I was trying to concentrate on an urgent fat-analysis, but people were shouting, running and screaming out in the passage. Then all of a sudden there was deadly quietness. I rushed to the door, just in time to escape a wave of fire that was making its way down the corridor. By the time I had reached safety half the factory was in flames. This incident led me to rededicate my life to God.

Healthwise it was not possible for me to continue with my chemistry career so my church suggested that I should go to Bible College. This I did with the intention of doing youth work in Germany after I had graduated. Never did I think that God would call me into missionary service.

The three fundamentals

Looking back I noticed three factors that were used by God to give me the assurance of His guidance: the Word of God, the inner witness of the Holy Spirit and outward circumstances.

The Word of God

Keeping a regular quiet time was one of the most important lessons I learned at Bible College. It was during those early hours in the morning that the Word of God became alive to me; the Lord started to speak and deal with things in my life. As I was studying Acts one day, a verse which I had read many a time suddenly hit me: 'Go, I will send you far away to the Gentiles' (Acts 22:21, NIV). I tried to push it away: 'Surely, the Lord can't possibly mean me? That was all right for Paul but certainly not for me,' I argued. A couple of days later another verse went right to my heart: 'I am sending you to them to open their eyes and turn them from darkness to light, and from the power of Satan to God' (Acts 26:17,18, NIV). Was the Lord really speaking to me? I had never shown any interest in missionary work. In fact I had tried to avoid any contact with missionaries. After all, my vision was to work among young people in Germany. So why bother about missions? But here was the Word of God speaking so clearly to me that I just had to accept. it.

The Inner Witness of the Holy Spirit

'You a missionary? You must be joking!' This was the reaction of my friends when I shared my conviction that God had called me. 'You can't have heard right. You will never make it healthwise,' I was told. So back I went to the Lord informing Him that it must have been a misunderstanding. But He would not let me get away with it and reconfirmed His calling to me by flooding my heart with His peace. Gone were all arguments that I was not suitable for missionary service. I could hardly believe it, but I was actually looking forward to it.

Circumstances

Now a lot of questions crowded my mind. What if I didn't pass my tropical medical? What missionary society should I join? And how about my mother? Would she let me go? My father had died soon after the war and I was the only child.

One by one I saw circumstances fall into place as I continued to trust the Lord. To my amazement my mother was overjoyed that I wanted to serve God on the mission field even though this would mean loneliness for her.

Unknown to me it had always been her own desire to become a missionary. I also learned for the first time that my parents had given me to the Lord as a tiny baby after I had been miraculously healed. So to my mother it was quite natural that God would want to use me in His service.

When I went for a check-up at the Tropical Institute I was quite apprehensive. The after-effects of chemical poisoning during my lab days had often bothered me. But that day I felt perfectly well and the doctor could not find anything wrong with me. He only advised me to have my kidneys tested before going to the tropics.

I still had no idea which missionary society to join. In fact, I didn't know any, since I had never been interested in missions before.

After my last term in Bible college, a friend asked me to hitchhike with her to Hamburg as she didn't want to spend all that money on fares for the long journey home. She arranged a place where we could stay overnight. It happened to be the German headquarters of WEC International! This mission had recently bought a house near Frankfurt. The small WEC team were just having their monthly prayer day. So we were invited to join them. The warm welcome and their love and openness soon made me feel at home. The homebase leader arranged for me to go to Scotland to work in the WEC missionary children's home. This not only gave me a chance to brush up on my English but also to learn more about WEC. Application papers to join the next candidate course in Germany reached me during my time in Scotland. The high standard of WEC principles presented quite a shock to me at first, but was turned by the

Lord into a challenge to learn how to depend on Him not only for spiritual needs but also for material ones.

My mother was in agreement with my going to the mission field; the tropical medicine exam was passed; and since the Lord had brought me into contact with a mission where I felt more and more at home, I knew it was right to apply for the WEC candidate course.

Obstacles in the way

Obstacles seem to be a common tool to prove our call into missionary service. I certainly got my share! My church (Lutheran) discouraged me from becoming a missionary; even my pastor did not think it was right for me.

Concerning the country to which I should go, I had my own ideas. Japan had always fascinated me. Since I had two Japanese penfriends I had been corresponding with regularly, I thought it quite in order for me to go to Japan as a missionary. Such were my naïve ideas of guidance. It would take a miracle from God to lead me to the country of His choosing!

After candidate course I was asked to go to England for further language study. But before I went I had to have my kidneys checked. The result of the test was shocking. I was told that my kidneys were in such a bad condition that I could never think of living in a tropical climate. My whole world collapsed! Had God not spoken to me after all? Had I just made it all up in my mind? I was utterly confused and went through a dark period of doubt not only regarding my calling into missionary service, but even about the reality of a living and caring God.

Medical miracle

Nevertheless I went to England and lived at the British headquarters, not telling anybody about my problems. I still continued having a daily quiet time mainly because it was expected of me. Nobody knew about my inner struggles. Out of desperation I cried to the Lord one day to speak to me again in my daily Bible reading. And God did speak! Not only did He reconfirm His calling through the life story of Abraham, but He also reminded me of His power that brought Lazarus back to life. Wouldn't I trust Him to use His lifegiving power to heal my kidneys? 'Me, a chemist, believe in miracles? Didn't God expect a bit too much of me?' For a whole week God challenged me to trust Him for healing until I hesitantly took this step of faith. But how was I to know if my kidneys were healed without having them checked again? I had to wait another three months until my English exams were over and I was back in Germany. Meanwhile God challenged me not only to believe Him but also to tell the WEC fellowship what He had done for me. That was the hardest bit of all. What if the kidney test did not show any signs of healing? It took more than my courage to share all this with the WEC family. How surprised I was that they reacted in such a positive and loving way, assuring me of their prayers.

During this time various missionaries from Thailand shared about their work. That was the last country I wanted to go to! I even had to look it up on the map to know where exactly it was. But here again God used His written Word and the inner witness of His Spirit to give me the assurance that Thailand was the country of His choice.

When I finally went back to Germany to have my kidneys checked everything was perfectly in order, to the amazement of the doctor, and to the glory of God!

In less than a year I was out in Thailand and I never regretted the Lord's choice. He gave me a deep love for the Thai and helped me to understand them and their way of thinking. Things weren't always easy, but then it was good to know that I hadn't chosen this country but that it was God's place for me.

There came a time when I had to leave Thailand for health reasons. Here again the Lord prepared me for this step by using the same principles: His Word, the inner witness of the Holy Spirit and outward circumstances. I certainly did not find it easy to go, not knowing what the future would hold, but it was another challenge to trust the Lord for fresh guidance.

[More recently Christel has served with WEC in Germany, promoting *Geared for Growth* Bible Studies.]

13

'Don't hedge — time flies!'

Rollie and Christina Grenier, Canada/Equatorial Guinea

By the grace of God my wife and I were saved in Lethbridge, Alberta through the witness and personal testimony of my brother John (presently a WEC missionary in The Gambia). Only months after our conversion, we could no longer see the sense of continuing with our regular jobs and lifestyle when we knew that millions around the world were dying without knowing the Saviour, Jesus. The Lord used our innocence as babes in Christ to let go of our jobs and begin a two year ministry in the inner-city of Winnipeg, Manitoba, amongst the abused and abusers of drugs, alcohol and sex.

Our pastor at that time, Jim Leverette, of Mission Baptist, Winnipeg, continued to challenge us and confirm our call to ministry and missions. During our time of preparation at Winnipeg Bible College opportunities came to us from all sides. Mission conferences brought us into contact with workers who could answer our questions. We eagerly invited many of these men and women into our homes to see what really made them 'tick'.

As visitors from a variety of missions kicked off their shoes and joined us in our living room I came to see that WEC missionaries were different. They had holes in their socks! I liked that because, as a student, so did I! They didn't have fancy suits or cars or even big elaborate display tables and brochures, but they had a special 'trust and obey' quality about them that attracted me. Many of them helped and guided us as we sought to discover God's place for us. In all of our times together I never sensed that they were specifically trying to recruit us for WEC, but rather helping us find where the Lord wanted us to serve.

Through a long and prayerful time of searching, we felt that the Lord was leading us to work with WEC reaching Spaniards for Christ. As we are a Spanish-speaking family we felt a joy and peace about taking this step of faith.

Prior to finishing Bible school, we had the privilege of getting to know an older WECer who had spent thirty years in South America – Wilf Watson. He was a man that we desired to be like, a man of deep commitment to God and a burning fire to complete the task of evangelising the world. Wilf was the first one to introduce us to the little known Spanish-speaking African country of Equatorial Guinea and challenged us to pray about the Lord leading us there. Despite the great need we couldn't imagine ourselves (at least my wife couldn't) going to Africa. Wilf encouraged us to go on to Spain but we kept our hearts open to Equatorial Guinea. Wilf's example of sacrificial giving, continuous prayer and spiritual insight made him a spiritual father to us.

The Lord did take us to Spain and just as we were settling in and seeking to find our niche in the team there, the Lord brought Equatorial Guinea to us again. The small team of five missionaries that had recently reopened the field after it being closed down for twenty-three years by the Marxist Macius Nguema government, was now down to one couple and they were leaving soon. The field would close if someone didn't fill the gap.

During the Spanish field conference, after hearing about the situation, Elliott Tepper, the founder of the Betel work in Spain, spoke with me saying 'We can't let Satan have the victory in this one'. Someone needed to go. As a couple we prayed to God, 'Why this, after bringing us to Spain? We have left everything to come here, and moreover, our church commissioned us to Spain, not to Africa.' We felt the Lord saying just to trust Him and obey. We thought that this maybe God's way of once again confirming our call to Spain, and putting our past doubts to rest, but may be not...

We prayed, 'Lord if we could just go and visit the work there we could pray more intelligently'. We thought that this was a safe prayer as our finances at the time were so low that it was impossible to make such a trip. The WEC family worldwide was praying about this urgent situation. Then we heard that a prayer group in western Canada was informing others that the Greniers were going to Guinea!

We received a call from Ron Brynjolfson, the outgoing field leader of Guinea at the time. He was excited about this 'news' and wanted to let us know that someone had designated funds for a survey trip. 'Trust and obey!'

Two weeks later Rob and myself arrived in Equatorial Guinea, right in the middle of governmental elections and divisions in the national church. The situation was so complex and desperate that after two weeks I felt sure that the Lord was reconfirming our call to Spain. I couldn't imagine Him sending us, as a family, to Guinea. I thanked God for the experience and returned to Spain with the answer – no. After sharing the situation with Cristina she looked me in the eye and said, 'If it is because you are afraid, that's not good enough'. We set a prayer goal for the end of the month, that the Lord would guide and give us peace regarding whatever the decision would be.

That month seemed to be the longest ever. We prayed, searched God's Word, received counsel, and pleaded that God would speak to both of us clearly. One weekend, near the end of the month, while staying at the mission's centre in Madrid, I couldn't sleep. I got up to pray and to read my Bible. Not wanting to waken Cristina I went into the office and turned on the light. On the desk in front of me was C.T.Studd's little book *The Chocolate Soldier*. I sat on the floor and began to read it. As I learned about the heroes of faith, tears came to my eyes. I yearned to be a man of faith and courage for the God Who had saved me through the death of His only Son, Jesus. As I dried my eyes I read the final page of the booklet. It said, 'To your knees, man! And to your Bible! Decide at once! Don't hedge! Time flies! Cease your insults to God. Quit consulting flesh and blood. Stop your lame lying and cowardly excuses. Enlist!'

The Lord had answered and we would enlist. God's promise was, 'I am with you always'. What more could we ask for?

The end of the month came and the Lord did give us that peace we sought after and on top of that He gave us such a joy in knowing and responding to His will. Hallelujah!

We were able to enter Equatorial Guinea and have the privilege of training young men and women in the Word of God in order to win Guinea for Christ. We could later see that the Lord did have a purpose in bringing us to Spain. It was there that He could speak to us, and where we could listen. The Lord also built up a strong prayer team in Spain and the national church has sacrificially given to the WEC work there.

[The Greniers are currently field leaders in Equatorial Guinea.]

14

Was it all for nothing?

Tineke Davelaar, Iran/Central Asia

Infectious enthusiasm

Very soon after my conversion, a deep longing came into my heart to know the Word of God better. Although I had attended the Dutch church from an early age and had gone to Christian schools, I knew that there was much more to discover. We had a Bible study group in the hospital where I was a student nurse. The person who taught us had a real heart for missions and she motivated us all to seek the Lord's will for our lives. She also shared with us information about missionaries and their work. This made a deep impression on me. The Lord opened the way for me to go to Bible college. For me that was the first step of faith. God had given me a desire to go and learn more about Him. During those first months a completely new world opened up for me.

Besides studying the Word of God and putting it into practice I had to unlearn many things through living with people from different backgrounds and cultures. I heard many missionary reports and testimonies. One of the girls with whom I shared a room, had been a missionary for many years in a Moslem land. She often shared her past experiences with me and would say, 'Let's pray together for the Moslems; evangelising these people is so difficult'. So we prayed together and God began to open my eyes to their need. My friend prayed in the meanwhile that God would call out labourers to work amongst them.

A year of Bible school training passed and for me the question became more urgent, 'Lord, what do you want me to do after my two years of training?' During the summer holidays I had more opportunity to seek the Lord quietly and He answered my prayer. It was faith-inspiring to read the well-known words from Psalm 139, 'Thou art acquainted with all my ways'. The Holy Spirit spoke directly to my heart that He would lead me out to the country of Iran and that I had to wait for His time. Joy and a great sense of wonder filled my heart; I knew God had spoken.

Oil, carpets and persian cats

I did not know much more about the country other than that it had oil, carpets and Persian cats. My interest was awakened; everything I could find about Iran I began to read, and I started writing to people working there.

My second year of Bible college seemed even more useful because I knew God had given me a sense of direction. But He had said that I should wait for His time and that was not always easy – or easily understood by others.

Three more years of preparation followed, in which I did further medical training. I also became involved in a local fellowship.

With what fellowship?
To me the big question was, 'With which missionary society should I go?' The counsel I had received urged me to go out with a fellowship; to go alone would be far too difficult. Looking back I am so glad of that advice!

So I began looking for missionary societies that were operating in Iran. I looked for organizations with long-term workers and finally I came to WEC. Joining a missionary society was a big step for me and I prayed much that God would lead me very clearly. Concerning WEC, the Lord spoke through Isaiah 48:17, 'I am the Lord... who teaches you what is best for you, who directs you in the way you should go'.

I felt immediately at home in the fellowship, knowing it to be God's will for me. At this stage, counsel from friends was not always positive. At one point I was even advised to consider another Moslem country, seeing that Iran had some missionary casualties. But the Lord encouraged me to cling to what He had said.

He told me that He would open the way in His good time.

So with more preparation, professional, mental and spiritual, and with praying people behind me, the door opened.

The first term was a time of much learning. Was my calling challenged? Yes, it was, and my faith was exercised: 'Lord, You have called; You have brought me here; You lead the way'.

Was it worth it?

Because of the revolution in Iran, my time lasted only four years or so. What I thought was to be a life-time work unexpectedly ended. Returning home the question came, 'Was it worth all the trouble – language learning, cultural adjustments – what was it all for, Lord?'

A few years later the answer came. He brought me in contact with Afghan and Iranian refugees in Holland! I could understand to a certain extent how difficult the adjustments to western culture were for them. Those contacts had a healing effect on me. After all, learning Farsi had not been in vain. As the Word says, 'God's ways are higher than ours'. No, He does not make mistakes, His way is perfect.

[Tineke served for several years as co-leader of one of WEC's Central Asian fields, and has recently been appointed co-director of candidate training for the Dutch sending base.]

15

I wasn't keen on Bible College

Elizabeth Stewart, Thailand

The power of prayer

My call to serve the Lord was the outcome of
over twenty years of prayer! Let me explain.
From my earliest childhood I have been aware
of the existence of God. Although my family
were regular attenders at an evangelical church
in Northern Ireland none of them had yet any
personal experience of salvation. What we didn't
know, however, was that a couple in that church
had been challenged by God some twenty years
previously to pray daily for us as a family. The
husband is now with the Lord but that widow
is still faithful to her promise and prays for me
every day. I was seventeen years old when I
became a Christian. Within the next couple of
years my mum, dad, sister and younger brother,
through varying circumstances, likewise came
to trust the Lord for salvation.

About a year after becoming a Christian, still
very young and unsteady in my faith, I went to
England to study at a college of education. Up
to this time I had never spoken openly about
my Christian experience – I considered this to

be something which was very personal, and so excused myself from sharing the 'Good News' with anyone else. When applying to various colleges it never occurred to me to seek the Lord's guidance concerning this. As I look back I can see how graciously and lovingly He did guide me at this very crucial stage. Just recently my mum told me that on the day she returned home from leaving me at the airport she said to my father, 'Elizabeth will never be back home with us for she'll be on the mission field some day'. At that time it was the last thing on my mind. But the Lord was already preparing my mum and dad for the day when I would leave for Thailand.

Progress during teacher training

Before leaving for college I had prayed very specifically that the Lord would give me Christian friends. This was probably the first time that I had been so definite in praying for anything and my prayer was very clearly answered. There were only about five or six other Christians amongst the first year students, but amazingly four of us met at a large central railway station before ever arriving at the college. Little did I imagine how important those four years were to be to my growth and development as a young Christian. The Christian Union was one of the smallest societies. However, this meant that all the members had to be fairly committed to all the activities – after all you couldn't skip even a prayer meeting without being missed and followed up. Consequently I soon found that all my spare time – apart from playing hockey – was given to Bible study groups, prayer meetings, discussion groups, outreach teams, etc. During this time I became aware that God had a purpose for my life. As I dedicated my life totally to Him I became increasingly aware of a desire to be involved in full-time Christian work. At this stage I still had no clear thought on where or even how I should serve the Lord, other than a very definite impression that this is what I should do.

At first I wanted to give up my teacher training and get out to the mission field; after all if this was the Lord's plan for my life then I wanted to get on with it. On sharing these thoughts with my minister he encouraged me but at the same time gave me some very wise counsel. He said that I shouldn't allow anything to distract me. I needed to prepare myself as adequately as possible both professionally and spiritually. Thus motivated, I went back to college and transferred to a degree course.

Putting God's will before qualifications

Two years later, with the same thought in mind, I returned to Ireland to teach for two years. Those two years at home were very precious to me. During this time I also became involved again with my local church as well as gaining valuable work experience. Teaching was for me the fulfilment of a childhood ambition and I enjoyed it tremendously. In fact at this stage it never occurred to me that I might serve the Lord in any capacity other than teaching. There was much prayer and heart searching as the Lord brought me to that point where I had to recognize that my obedience and availability to Him was more important than qualifications. I realized that I had to be willing even if it meant I was never to teach again, or indeed be willing to stay at home should He lead that way. All this came to a head because I knew that the Lord was directing me to study at the Faith Mission Bible College in Edinburgh, Scotland.

In all honesty while I knew very little about the Faith Mission or the Bible College, this wasn't the type of training that I had envisaged – character training, strict discipline, set uniform. At college it was continually emphasized that more important than anything else was getting to know God and maintaining a daily relationship with Him.

Problems

After being accepted for Bible college there were still two issues about which I was greatly concerned. Firstly, there was the problem of my health. I suffered quite badly from rheumatoid arthritis and really feared that no missionary society in its right mind would even consider me as a candidate. Yet I felt absolutely sure that it was right for me to prepare for service. Secondly, I was very concerned about my family. At the time my mum was extremely ill; how could it be right to go when they needed me? The thing that sticks most in my memory about this period was the amount of time I spent in prayer – and in tears – before the Lord. I desperately wanted to follow what I believed to be the Lord's will for my life but how could I? Someone from my church even suggested that my going away could be more than my mum could bear. However the Lord constantly brought me back to Matthew 6:33, 'Seek ye first the Kingdom of God and all these things shall be added unto you'.

The process of finding God's will

Initially I was only aware of a desire to serve the Lord but as I began to move in this direction other things gradually began to come into focus. During the first few months of Bible college, as the Holy Spirit worked in my life, I found there was a shift in my thinking – not so much what I was going to do for the Lord but rather what the Lord was wanting to do in my life. It is all too easy to insist on following our own ambitions and desires while yet at the same time claiming the Lord's guidance for our actions. One thing we can always be sure of is, that the

Lord's guidance will never be inconsistent with the teaching of His own Word. It was only after I came to the point where I confessed to the Lord a heart desire for His will and not my own selfish ambitions that He began to show me the way ahead. Many fears and obstacles were cleared aside. For example, one Sunday afternoon Rev. Arthur Neil, the principal of the college, prayed with me for healing. Within a few days all the pain and stiffness had gone – completely.

Over the months I began to realize that my thoughts and prayers were more and more turning to Asia and in particular to Thailand. At one point it seemed that almost every book, missionary article, or magazine that I picked up had a reference to Thailand. One night as I was reading Isaiah 6 I was thinking of Isaiah's commission to serve the Lord. I simply said to the Lord, 'Well, here I am, I want to go and proclaim the Gospel but please show me to which peoples I am to go'. As I picked up a few books from my bed my eye caught a notice on the back cover of a WEC magazine: 'Wanted urgently – Teachers in Thailand'. Could this be confirmation of what I was thinking about? Was it a word from the Lord? Or was it just what I was wanting to see?

These questions were very much in my mind as I had my quiet time next morning. I was feeling a little frustrated because in my morning readings I was presently working through the book of Chronicles. Of all books, how could the Lord use this to speak to my heart? But God did speak to me through 1 Chronicles 28:10, 'Take heed now; for the Lord has chosen you...' And then in verse 20: 'Be strong and courageous and do the work. Do not be afraid or discouraged for the Lord God, my God is with you. He will not fail you or forsake you.'

Probing the principles and practices of mission groups

With this assurance I proceeded to the next step. I found out all I could about the different missionary societies working in Thailand. After prayerful consideration of their principles and practices, together with the type of work being done, I felt that there were two missions with whom I could work equally well. I was looking for a society who lived according to faith principles. It just happened that both these societies had organized house-parties in the Edinburgh area around that time. The WEC one came up first. I was very impressed by the caring atmosphere and lovely spirit that I sensed there. Within my spirit I felt a oneness with this group and a witness that this was the one for me. However, I wanted to double check and to give the other group an equal opportunity. Although the second house-party was addressed by an internationally renowned speaker – someone whose books I had devoured for years – the Holy Spirit still witnessed in my heart that WEC was the organization for me. As a result, soon after this, I applied for work in Thailand.

On the morning that the application papers arrived I asked the Lord to give me a word of confirmation. After the coffee break, classes resumed with a lecture on the Minor Prophets. Almost out of context for the class but very much in context for me, the lecturer began to speak about being obedient to the Lord's voice. He said, 'Many of you folks will find yourselves serving the Lord here in Scotland, in Ireland or England or perhaps Africa or India'. He paused and then added, 'Perhaps there is even someone here who will go to Thailand'. Because of the timing of this comment, less than fifteen minutes after I had asked for confirmation, I took this to be a further word from the Lord.

Parents in pain

As I neared the end of my candidate course I was painfully aware how much my decision was costing the family. I was very upset when my mum announced on one occasion that she didn't think it was the Lord's will for me to go to Thailand. I knew that they would never stop me going but I so wanted them to have the Lord's peace about this too. The night before my final acceptance into WEC I rather shocked one of the staff. She was joking with me, 'By

this time tomorrow you'll be in'. I burst into
floods of tears. After we had prayed and talked
together I phoned my parents. My mum assured
me that while she didn't like to see her daughter
going so far away she knew within her heart
that this was right and that what she had said
previously was an emotional reaction. I am so
thankful to the Lord for my family, for their
loving support and their faithful prayers. There
is no doubt in my mind that the sacrifices and
the pain of parting is greater for parents than it
is for the young missionary going out, full of
zeal and excitement.

A sense of proportion, not panic

When I finally arrived, it was the Lord's time. I
was very glad that I was so sure of my guidance
before setting out. The first few months were
very difficult – learning one of the world's most
difficult languages, experiencing home-sickness
and culture shock, and then, following a bout
of dengue fever, the arthritis flared up again. This
shook me not only physically but also spiritually
and emotionally. The Lord had healed so why
did it re-occur? My problem was increased by
some insensitive words of advice and counsel.
There were those who suggested that this
indicated that I was out of the Lord's will by
being in Thailand. Others suggested that it was
due to my lack of faith or because of some
unconfessed sin or perhaps it was from Satan

and as such had to be denied. God had called me here, of that I was sure, so what was going on? Had He forgotten about me?

God reminded me that it was He Who had 'suggested' that I go to Thailand and that it was He Who had promised that He would never leave me nor forsake me. Although I didn't know all the answers, I could still trust Him. Many times I have had to go back to this lesson and ask the Lord to help me keep things in perspective, to get them back in proportion, to see it from God's 'point of view'.

Looking back I would say that even more important than how God has used my life in Thailand has been how God has used Thailand in my life.

[Elizabeth is currently leader of the Thailand field.]

16

No regrets

Irene Höft, Thailand

Airline hostess-to-be

Do you enjoy a lukewarm cup of coffee? Maybe some people do, but certainly not the Europeans.

My Christianity was just like that – lukewarm, and I didn't enjoy it. I came to know Christ in my teens during my studies in Syracuse, New York. It was a time when my imagination made vivacious escapades about life's future career. As an extrovert I enjoyed people, wanted to study different nationalities and had little difficulty adapting to new cultures. I am German but I enjoyed the American way of life. My dream was to become a glamorous airline hostess. I was good at languages – English, French, Latin and of course German. I had a strong desire to explore the world into which I was born. So God had already laid a foundation for my future.

But soon my dreams were shattered. Disillusionment filled my heart and mind as I returned to Germany to continue studies and then work at the head office of the Deutsche Bank in Hamburg. As I analysed the monotony of my own lifestyle and that of my colleagues there, I realised the vanity and aimlessness of it all. I seemed to be drifting from one day to the next, one month to the next, waiting for wages and then spending money all too rapidly. Was this life? Work just to survive, mixed with a little pleasure here and there? Although I was a so-called Christian the vacuum within me grew from week to week, especially after I was invited to attend church by my sister-in-law.

Sunday after Sunday God's two-edged sword pierced my heart, causing great conflicts within me. All my rational excuses seemed to lose their foundation. I knew something had to change. After only nine months at the bank, I put in my resignation. This left the manager completely speechless. I had been a competent worker and had great opportunities for promotion. Yet the decision to leave was already made in the depth of my heart. No enticing offer could change it.

A vacuum

I, who loved to make plans, suddenly had no prospects. What would my parents say to this quick decision? My father was still in the States. When he heard this news he was furious and thought I was mentally unstable – a religious fanatic.

What would be my next step? Everything was uncertain. The only thing I knew was that I had resigned and had no other work. God used mum to support me, and encouraged me to write to an Evangelistic Crusade, the Janz Brothers, who had their headquarters in South Germany, 800 kms from home. But my enquiry about work received a negative reply. They would take note of my name, but no vacancies were available. Doubt and confusion entered my mind. Had I not made the decision trusting the Lord to open a new door? It was quite impossible just to sit at home. Yet I couldn't see any other way. Days of intensive prayer and searching God's Word followed. I clung to the truth that He would guide His people. Although I was not a strong Christian, I knew God had to fulfil His promises.

All of a sudden the doors opened. The Janz Brothers wrote asking me to join them in the beginning of the new year. My heart rejoiced. God proved to be faithful. He wanted me to learn to trust Him in patience as He promised in Psalm 66:19, 20. This period with the Janz Brothers was used by God to stabilize my faith. I was asked to give my first testimony. I refused at first, because I hadn't the faintest idea how to do it; besides I was much too shaky and shy to stand in front of all those spiritual people at the Baptist Church in Lorrach. Yet they insisted. So I was cast on the Lord for His instruction.

While I was asking the Lord for a word, the Holy Spirit led me to Ezekiel 3:16-19. I had never read this passage before. As I stood in front of the congregation and read God's Word I could hardly swallow. My knees were shaking, I hardly dared to look up as they stared at me in silence. I thought they had all left the place, but as I finally finished reading and looked up, they were all weeping. So was I. The words in verse 18 kept echoing in my ears '...if you don't warn him (the sinner) he will die... I will hold you responsible for his death'.

A proposal of marriage

This incident changed my life. I knew I had to go and tell the Good News. But I was not prepared to go to Bible college because I was plagued by severe migraine and headaches. How could I concentrate on studies? That was, of course, a very reasonable excuse. On the other hand I had just received a marriage proposal from a theologian who had finished five years at a famous theological college in Switzerland. Somehow I couldn't say 'yes'. In fact I said 'no' to this proposal without any hesitation, but I still was not willing to go and study. Restlessness pursued me until I finally bargained with God. 'If You want me to go to Bible college, then You just have to take these headaches away.' And God did. So I had to keep my word and go, but never with the intention of going to the mission field.

Upon entering Bible college I wrote in my diary, 'We are guided by God, even if we are not aware of it'.

This truth proved to be a tremendous guideline, especially in times of indecisiveness and confusion. Something that agitated me in Bible college was that nearly all of my classmates knew that God wanted them to be missionaries. I knew nothing. My mind was blank. I couldn't picture myself being a missionary – even when for two years I was chosen secretary of the student mission board and had a chance to go to two big student missionary conferences in Brussels and Lamorlaye, Paris. It wasn't that I was rebellious, but I simply didn't sense the call to be a missionary. When Brother Andrew challenged the many students to be prepared to enter China, as God has no closed doors, I also raised my hand. Yet inwardly I knew it was not really a commitment.

From confusion to clarity

As secretary of the European Student Mission Association for Germany I needed to be informed about mission societies and the lives of missionaries, so I had to read missionary books. One by Isobel Kuhn *Ascent to the Tribes*, impressed me. Without realizing it I started to pray faithfully for the tribal people in Northern Thailand. Yet it never entered my mind that God wanted me to be a missionary in that country. In my last year at a conference with Corrie ten Boom I was asked the usual question – what would I do? I still couldn't give a specific answer. One of the conference visitors seemed to be quite disturbed that I was so vague about my future. She prodded me by asking if there was any country to which I would very much like to go. I couldn't really answer her in a positive way. 'Don't you have a burden for something?' she continued. Her motivating questions made me realize that I *did* have a burden – a prayer burden for Northern Thailand. 'Why don't you specifically ask the Lord to make it clear to you if this is the country of His choice for your future?' she continued. I really had to ask myself, 'Did I want to be a missionary?' I felt so inadequate to lead a life of sacrifice, but the more I concentrated on this specific prayer, the more peace and clarity filled my heart and mind.

Before my graduation two major incidents happened which gave me inner confirmation of God's wonderful provision, and strengthened my faith in Him. Moved by a profound hunger for more of God's reality and His power in our lives, a small group of us students started to meet regularly for prayer. Unexpectedly God visited us and filled our lives with His transforming power in a new way. A few days after that He also healed me of an infirmity which had plagued me for a long time. These experiences destroyed a lot of my fears and inadequacies.

More confirmation

Yet my faith continued to be tested in various ways. During the interim period after training, doubt about this strange country crept subconsciously into me. I asked the Lord to confirm again to me that this was His way for me. And He again proved to be faithful, like He was to Gideon. Prayer news for different countries around the world was sent to me each month. On my birthday, the first of February, I wanted Thailand to be the country to be prayed for. It sounds like a silly small thing, yet to me it wasn't. Can you imagine how my hands trembled when I received the prayer calendar on January 30th? Here it was in big black letters – 1 February: Thailand. Tears of joy and praise filled my heart. What an understanding Heavenly Father we have!

But the testing was not over. I applied to a certain missionary society but the conditions laid down caused me to question whether this was God's choice for me.

After I had made a definite break with that society, the wife of the State Church pastor suggested that I contact WEC. I did and an interview was arranged, which proved to be most disappointing; the leader gave me nothing specific to cling to. 'Well,' he casually mentioned, 'if the Lord really wants you to join us, He will make it clear to you and to us.' Honestly! Such vagueness! Here I was at the end of my working period with the State Church and had to return home with no future plans. 'What a crazy mixed-up life of uncertainties,' they would surely think. I knew the next candidate course was not too far away. Three long weeks of waiting and intense prayer followed.

Finally the desired letter arrived with the invitation to join the next course. Surely now the way would be without obstacles and I would be in Thailand in a short time.

Only a few weeks at the German WEC headquarters had elapsed when unexpected news about the sudden death of my sister reached me. It shook my entire family. I knew my mother needed my moral and spiritual support at this time. Was God redirecting my way? Friends, who had previously supported my going into the mission, commented that it would be quite unloving to leave mum now. As I pondered upon this, I had to agree. I claimed God's guidance and asked Him to make me willing to abandon my plans to go to Thailand. As I brought the entire matter before His throne one day, a distinct inner voice asked me, 'Do you think you can care for mum better than I can? Are you willing to leave her in My hands?' I knew it was the Master's voice. How could I have doubted His care for mum? So I returned to headquarters, finished the six months course, collected as much information about Thailand as possible and got ready to go.

A final hurdle

I had no query about my physical fitness because I had had a check-up at the tropical institute at Tubingen, Germany. Meanwhile it was arranged that another female candidate and I visit various churches. Just before we went off one of the staff members passed a letter to me from Tubingen. I didn't pay much attention as I somehow knew I was fit, but something prompted me to open the letter. I couldn't believe what it said. The institute didn't feel I was fit and therefore did not recommend that the mission send me out. I felt a knife piercing through me. What was God doing? I just didn't comprehend! And in a few hours I was to testify of His call and confirmation to go to Thailand! As I picked up my friend's Bible just next to me, I cried to the Lord in anxiety to give me a specific word for this situation. The Bible fell open to Psalm 55:22, 'Cast your problems (troubles) on the Lord, and He will sustain you'. I did just exactly that, and the burden left. That night as I shared my unfitness with brothers and sisters, an elderly brother stood up, embraced me, and said, 'Sister, the Lord just wants to pour

His fitness and strength into you'. What an encouragement!

And God kept His word again. The mission never mentioned anything about this letter. Only a few days prior to my final departure did the leader mention it, but they too realized that God's approval stood above human infirmities.

In my years of service in Thailand the road has not been smooth. In fact, the first term was full of conflicts, doubts and uncertainties. Often I wanted to pack my suitcase, but it seemed that a stronger hand was holding me.

I have learned that disappointments will never cease if I concentrate on seeking the fulfilment of my merely human longings. But if my essential longings lead me to seek that Person, that Someone Whose purposes are supremely important, then the profound desires of my soul will be satisfied. His infinite love is unconditional.

17

A bumpy ride

Barbara Scott, Chad/Senegal

I'm not following someone else's footsteps!
'One day you will be a missionary like your
parents,' remarked a well-meaning elderly lady.
'No, never – I'm not following in someone else's
footsteps,' was the reply of the rebellious
teenager. 'Why should people take things for
granted?' My parents might have been
missionaries and I admired them for it. Jesus was
my Saviour – I'd given my life to Him at the age
of twelve – but there it ended. I would choose
my own way.

It was at the age of fifteen, during a Bible
study, that God started speaking to my heart
through John 20:21, 'As the Father has sent me,
I am sending you', linked with Isaiah 61:1, 2. I
knew deep down that God loved me and He
wanted me to reach out to those around and
share His love with them. Five years later, being
in my final year of nursing studies, owning a
wee car, thoroughly enjoying life, involved in a
church, God challenged me once again. I was at
a missionary conference (at the WEC centre in
Kilcreggan) and every time missionaries spoke I
knew God wanted me to give my life one day

in service for Him, but though five years back I'd said 'yes' now I was afraid of really making Him Lord of my life, afraid of all He might ask me to give up, like my car, or my nursing. I had no peace but was able to talk it all through with a missionary – June Hobley from Liberia. Constantly the verse of the hymn came to me – 'There is no peace, no joy, no thrill like walking in His will...' and when I totally surrendered to the Lord, peace came.

Too hard for God?

The Lord slowly started challenging me through books and missionary messages about the needs in Moslem countries. Reading Charles Marsh's book *Too Hard for God?* all of a sudden I came across the country of Chad and was stopped in my tracks. What was Chad? Where was it? Who worked there? As I discovered the answers to my questions and started praying and corresponding with missionaries there, the conviction came that this was the country to which God was calling me. I found out that WEC worked in Chad, and God showed me that He wanted me to go to the WEC Missionary Training College in Glasgow. During my first year, Chad missionaries came and spoke, and yet I still wondered if this really was what God had for me. Through verses in Psalm 37 He often spoke saying that this was the land He had given me to possess. I still lacked assurance, then one night I read Psalm 32:8, 9: 'I will instruct you and teach you in the way you should go; I will counsel you and watch over you. Do not be like the horse or the mule, which have no understanding but must be controlled by bit and bridle.' God's quiet voice spoke again. 'I've confirmed it time and time again – will you be like a mule without understanding?' Peace came as I said, 'I'll go Lord'.

Following MTC I had my plans laid out: candidate course, French language school in Switzerland, then Chad. But my ways were not God's. At my interview I was told the candidate course would be postponed for six months, due to lack of numbers. What would I do? My plans went upside down and I found that hard. At my interview I said I would go to France and start studying, but I knew no-one there and I knew no French. God's still small voice came through again 'Only in acceptance lies peace' and I knew He would work it out. Within a few weeks I was at a medical centre on the outskirts of Paris, working as a district nurse and learning French... not my way, but God's. I'd been dropped from French classes at school, told that I could never learn a language, and that I would have a mental block if sent to a language school, so He threw me in at the deep end, having to pick up the language as I worked! He kept me there eighteen months.

All change, in Chad

Candidate course passed, then deputation and farewells. I arrived in Chad and knew that deep sense of peace that I had arrived 'home'. A second language had to be faced – Arabic. Rebel activity intensified and we finally had to leave the country. My mind questioned 'What are You doing, Lord? You called me to Chad, and I love it. Why did we have to leave?' I always expected to return and felt it would be a great help to have some further Arabic studies, so went to Jordan for a term. Later, I was all set for a return but a few days before I left Britain, war broke out again... I had planned a visit to Senegal en route, so what now? In a prayer meeting a missionary who had visited Senegal happened to say 'If you are a nurse, have French and Arabic, you are needed to reach the Mauritanians'. He did not know I was there, and he later could not even remember saying those words, but God planted the seed thought in my heart of reaching Mauritanian people from a base on Senegal's border.

Moving to the Maures

After waiting for three months and seeing that Chad was not settling I then moved to Senegal to give six months to reaching Maures. The local trade language in Senegal is Wolof and I needed that before adapting my Arabic to Mauritanian Arabic. So I gave a full three years to a small

Mauritanian village, living closely with the people. As time came for furlough the question was asked 'What are you going to do – return to Chad, where the team was building up again and nurses were needed, or return to Senegal, to Maure work?' Having adapted to the local Arabic, I became involved in the ministry of evangelism. Knowing that deep sense of peace that I had been in the right place, I felt I should return to Senegal. Towards the end of my furlough the Lord reconfirmed this through His Word. Once again in John 20:21, 'As the Father sent me, I am sending you'. Then the words of Peter in Luke 5:5, 'Master, we've worked hard all night and haven't caught anything, but because You say so, I will let down the nets'. I knew that I should return to Senegal and that the Lord was promising to give fruit.

Looking back at the way God has led me to the mission field, three factors have been important:

* The principles of God's Word,
* The prompting of the Holy Spirit,
* The providences of life.

My response had been the words of 2 Samuel 15:15, 'Your servants are ready to do whatever our Lord the King chooses.'

18

I didn't need flashing lights

Robyn Lanham, Japan/Australia

What led me to the mission field? A divinely-appointed set of 'coincidences'.

The tantrum thrower

For as long as I can remember, I've always had an interest in Japan. One aunt informed me that she recalls asking me what I was going to be when I grew up. 'A missionary in Japan' was the reply. How a painfully shy untidy six-year-old tantrum-thrower could know that, before the Lord took her in hand three years later at a Billy Graham Crusade, only the Lord Himself knows.

Growing up in a Christian home with a godly mum and dad meant that I always expected the Lord to have a specific plan for my life and to reveal it to me step by step. So it was no surprise to end up with numerous Japanese penfriends, even though I'd specifically applied for French penfriends on whom to practise my high school French!

My first recollection of that interest in Japan was in my first year at high school. I attended an Inter-Schools Christian Fellowship camp for girls at the Blue Mountains in Australia. My dorm leader 'just happened' to be a furloughing OMF missionary from Japan.

In those days, the verses which held specific meaning for me as a teenager were Romans 12:1,2 which taught me that God's good and acceptable and perfect will for my life was inextricably bound up with presenting my body to HIM for HIM to use, not in tuning in to the world. What a 'coincidence' to receive a letter from my OMF friend, now back in Japan, with Romans 12:1,2 quoted in full at the top of her letter!

I remember attending numerous missionary meetings in my high school days (mostly focussing on New Guinea) and coming home freshly amazed and excited over God's 'coincidences': either the message was based on Romans 12:1,2 (which now held a certain Japanese flavour for me), or there was a clear reference to Japan during the evening (which reminded me of Romans 12:1,2), or both. By the end of high school days, it had happened so often that I had absolutely no doubt whatever that these were the gentle nudgings of my Heavenly Father concerning His specific plan for my life.

Marriage not a substitute for obedience

There was however, one big problem. Would-be-missionaries who are so shy that they find it impossible to open their mouths, even to share their testimony, need special training. I didn't have a clue what the Lord wanted me to do between high school and Bible college. After praying and asking God to lead me aright by closing all the wrong doors and opening the right one, I applied for various scholarships. Only one possibility came out of that: a scholarship enabling me to train as a high school teacher of commercial subjects. Me? A high school teacher? You've got to be kidding. Teachers have to open their mouths! But what better preparation for this would-be-missionary? His ways ARE much higher than ours.

During those two years of training and four years of experience the Lord gave me a deep love for teaching. As well, the series of quiet 'coincidences' continued, mostly involving Romans 12:1,2 and Japan. How I praise Him in retrospect that Japan was a settled issue already by then. It held me firmly when the good alternatives of marriage and settling down became a strong option. I knew deep down that to go that way would be disobedience, and His Spirit gave no peace. I knew without a shadow of doubt that marriage – even to a Christian – was not a substitute for obedience.

Before I entered teachers training college, my parents had attended a Christian Endeavour Convention on the other side of Australia – at Victor Harbour, south of Adelaide. When they returned they said, 'When you go to college, we'd be thrilled if you went to that one at Victor Harbour'. Six years later, when the time came to apply for training those words came back to me with such force that I knew it was the Lord's voice. How I praise Him for parents who encouraged me positively in His way. I never knew how hard it would be for them until the day I left for Japan. My mum, choked up with the inevitable tears that airports produce, handed me a note. I read it on the plane. 'I know whom I have believed and am convinced that He is able to guard what I have entrusted to Him until that day.'

More coincidences

His divinely-planned 'coincidences' followed me to Bible college. My first year coincided with the third year of a Japanese student, now Pastor Kazuo Sekine. My second and third years overlapped with the first and second years of another Japanese student, who became a special friend, and whose spiritual birthday happened to be the same day as my birthday!

During second year, our principal encouraged us not to wait until just before the graduation before asking the Lord concerning specific guidance for the future. I had no doubts about 'where'. That was an unshakeable conviction by now. But I had to admit that 'with whom' was just an assumption on my part. All my contact through the years had been with OMF, so I assumed I would automatically go to Japan with that mission. But years of familiarity with Biblical principles made me wary of the dangers of assumptions! David hadn't automatically assumed God's guidance (1 Chronicles 14:8-17). As a result he won two resounding victories. I knew that two of Israel's biggest defeats under Joshua's leadership came because they assumed God was with them and didn't enquire from the Lord in specific situations (Joshua 7 and 9).

So I set about asking the Lord 'with whom?' I selected the three mission societies that I knew worked in Japan – OMF, WEC, and TEAM – and then asked the Lord to confirm the one of His choice by a certain date. From the time I began to pray, until that date, WEC came up over and over again – 'coincidence' after 'coincidence'. Visiting WEC missionaries, (including one from Japan), WEC literature, a visit by the WEC representative of South Australia to college, etc., all were links in the chain. It was only added confirmation when I received a letter from my pastor one day strongly advising one of the other two missions. If it had come before the deadline, what confusion! But coming one day after, it only served to test what the Lord had already confirmed.

God never wastes experiences. What is a teacher of shorthand, typing and accounting doing in Japan? What an unbelievable help it has been over the years, knowing the principles of teaching and being able to use shorthand. It all helped in learning some of those squiggles that make up the Japanese written language and in pronouncing the spoken language. And what better experience is needed when I had to stand in for the secretary/treasurer when she went on furlough? And how I've praised the Lord that He opened my mouth! I love teaching the Japanese and seeing them grow in response to Biblical and spiritual truths. This was something my high school students never did, in response to my teaching them shorthand, typing and book-keeping!

A confession

Now I have a confession to make. Until I came to write this testimony, I've had a sneaking suspicion that reliance on 'coincidences' is not very spiritual; that the most spiritual way to be led by the Lord is to experience loud thunderclaps, flashes of lightning, audible voices, and if still the Lord can't quite get our honourable attention, the spiritual sledge hammer. But already I've thought of three Bible stories which would have had different endings if there hadn't been a divinely-planned coincidence.

A king with insomnia and a tyrant nursing a grudge just happen to be in the right place at the right time (Esther 6:1-12).

Another king who loved hearing true stories, a dead prophet's servant who enjoyed telling true stories, and the heroine of one of those stories all put in their appearance at just the right time (2 Kings 8:1-6).

A foreigner gleaning in the right field at just the right time (Ruth 2:1-3).

There are probably lots more. My dictionary tells me that a coincidence is a 'circumstance agreeing with another, often implying accident'. But my God doesn't do things by accident; He causes 'ALL things to WORK TOGETHER for good to those who love God, to those who are called according to His purpose'. And that includes me!

[Robyn is currently candidate director at WEC's Australian headquarters in Sydney.]

19

Thirty steps for serious seekers

Many excellent books deal with the Biblical principles of guidance. Our purpose is simply to lay out briefly a number of practical steps – illustrated in the stories already given – that can be taken by the serious seeker after God's specific purpose.

1. **WITHDRAW** from all known sin. We can't expect to have our prayers answered if we have not dealt with unconfessed sin. Isaiah tells us that sin separates us from God (Isaiah 59:1, 2). So, confess it, and seek God's will as a cleansed person. John says in his First Epistle that God 'is faithful and just and will forgive us our sins and purify us' if we come in genuine confession (1 John 1:9).

2. **WILLINGNESS** to submit to the Lord's direction. We must first settle the issue of commitment to discipleship and be willing to accept the principle of the cross as Christ explains in Luke 14:27; 'Anyone who does not carry his cross and follow me cannot be my disciple.'

3. **WANT** to know. What is your heart's desire? Is the will of God your highest priority? Jesus says, 'Seek first the kingdom' in Matthew

6:33 and promises that if we do this all the things that we normally consider as priorities – the 'basics' of living – will be given to us.

4. **WAIT** on God. This involves keeping the matter consistently before God in prayer, and thinking things through in His presence. Acts 13 describes how a group of men decided to fast and wait in God's presence. As they did so the Holy Spirit showed them what to do (vv. 1-3).

5. **WHOLEHEARTED** trust. Proverbs 3:5-6 says: 'Trust in the Lord with all your heart... in all your ways acknowledge him and he will make your paths straight. Do not be a 'double-minded man, unstable in all he does' (James 1:8). Trust God implicitly and totally.

6. **WEAR** Christ's yoke. Christ invites us to share a yoke with Him (Matthew 11:29). What is the significance? A yoke is a device for keeping two animals together as they pull a plough. In practice, a less experienced animal learns from its partner a) through close contact, b) by being guided in the right direction, c) by moving forward at the right pace. The spiritual application is obvious.

7. **WORD** of God. The Holy Spirit will never lead you contrary to the truths of God's Word. The Psalmist says, 'I have hidden your word in my heart that I might not sin against you' (Psalm 119:11). Beware of isolating special verses and taking them as 'guidance'.

8. **WEIGH** the circumstances. Remember Satan's purpose is to hinder and deflect us from God's will, as Paul infers in 1 Thessalonians 2:18. And remember too that Satan has evil spirits who want to lead us astray (1 Timothy 4:1). So learn how to interpret the happenings of life while being sensitive to the Holy Spirit.

9. **WISDOM** of counsellors. Share your concern with spiritually-minded seniors whose opinion you value. Very often confirmation comes through their reaction or advice. 'A wise man listens to advice' (Proverbs 12:15).

10. **WAYS** of guidance for others. Study the manner in which God has guided His servants. You will find many instances in Scripture, church history and biography. Take note of the experiences of modern disciples like Brother Andrew, Dr Helen Roseveare and Bruce Olsen.

11. **WETTING** of the fleece. When it is hard to distinguish between personal feelings and the Spirit's confirmation, ask God to do something objective outside yourself, as an indication of His will. Gideon was very unsure, so he asked God to cause a fleece which he placed on the threshing floor overnight to be covered with dew next morning, and the surrounding area to be dry. It happened. Next night he reversed the request and that happened too (Judges 6:37-39).

12. **WRITE** out a balance sheet. It is good to sit down with a sheet of paper divided into two

columns and list the reasons for and against taking a particular decision.

13. **WIN** a prayer partner (or group). If the issue is of long term significance, it is an excellent idea to share your need with someone who will stand with you in positive faith for God's mind to be revealed. 'For where two or three come together in my name, there am I with them' (Matthew 18:20).

14. **WORK** to establish spiritual principles. Often specific guidance is not needed because the issue is covered by a biblical principle. For example, 'Obey your leaders' (Hebrews 13:17) and 'Seek first the Kingdom' (Matt. 6:33), 'If you forgive... your heavenly Father will forgive you' (Matt.6:14), 'First be reconciled' (Matt.5:24).

15. **WATCH** for the Spirit's equipment. This is specially relevant to those concerned about Christian service. The Holy Spirit's gifts can be an indication of the avenue you should take.

16. The **WITNESS** of the Holy Spirit. The Holy Spirit confirms by an inner assurance what God is showing you in other ways. At the same time beware of a peace which is simply the absence of tension following a time of decision-making.

17. **WAGE WAR** against selfish desires. Beware of decisions that are dominated by the desire for affluence, ease or the fulfilment of personal ambitions. Paul warns the Romans, 'Do

not conform any longer to the pattern of this world' (12:2).

18. Be **WARY** of counterfeits. Often the good is the enemy of the best. For example, don't make the excuse that the choir can't manage without you if the Holy Spirit is convincing you about going to Bible college.

19. The **WORLD** can allure. Ensure that your decision is not dominated by a desire for position, security or acclaim. 1 John 2:16 identifies the world with 'the cravings of sinful man, the lust of his eyes and the boasting of what he has and does'.

20. **WATCH** the subtlety of the rational mind. Don't tackle a spiritual issue with humanistic resources. Proverbs 3:5 warns us about being dependent on our own understanding.

21. **WISDOM** that is sanctified and used with spiritual discernment can help determine the right course. For instance, Paul saw Timothy's potential as a future Christian worker and asked him to join his team (Acts 16:1-3).

22. **WITHSTAND** fear. 'Perfect love drives out fear' (1 John 4:18). God is a loving heavenly Father. His will is the best thing that could happen to us. What to fear most is moving outside the security of His perfect will.

23. **WEAKNESS** does not disqualify. Christians often resist God's will because they don't feel adequate for that to which God is

calling them. But His commission carries the guarantee of His enabling. In Philippians 4:13 Paul says, 'I can do everything through him' and Hebrews 13:20, 21 says, 'May the God of peace... equip you with everything good for doing his will'.

24. **WORLD** need and Christ's command about meeting that need with the message of the gospel, as stated in Matthew 28:18-20, constitute a general principle of guidance for every Christian. Once the principle is accepted the issues of how to serve, where to serve, and with whom to serve can become matters for specific direction.

25. **WAITING** in complete passivity is not biblical. Guidance won't just 'arrive'. Use the means given in a positive way. Psalm 32:9 says, 'Do not be like the horse or mule, which have no understanding but must be controlled by bit and bridle.'

26. **WORKING** to a deadline can be a healthy exercise. If the answer is needed by a certain date, confidently assert your expectancy that the Lord will give an indication of His will by that time. Jesus sets the pattern in Mark 11:24, 'Whatever you ask for in prayer, believe that you have received it, and it will be yours.'

27. **WALK** by faith. Be prepared to step out in faith. If you know God has given a sense of direction, then the only course is to launch out,

trusting Him implicitly. As Jesus said to Peter in Luke 5:4, 'Put out into deep water.'

28.God **WANTS** to guide you! In fact He can't stop being in sovereign control of your life! And if in His wisdom He puts you temporarily into a bit of darkness He will expect you to walk by faith through it. See Isaiah 50:10-11.

29.**WAITING** may be your biggest trial. God may have something to TEACH you before you are in a condition for Him to SHOW you. Or perhaps a new set of circumstances needs to fall into place before He can reveal the step you should take. Study the events in Acts 16:6-15.

30.**WORK** towards CONSENSUS if you are a member of a group seeking God's purpose. The goal is to reach a point where 'the peace of God' is the 'referee' in your hearts. See Colossians 3:15.

51 books that deal with guidance

Adeney M. *A Time for Risking. A Challenge to Women* Multnomah: Portland, OR, 1987

Anderson N.T. *Walking in the Light. Discerning God's Mind in the New Age* Here's Life: San Bernardino 1993, Monarch: Tunbridge Wells

Barclay. O. *Guidance, Some Biblical Principles* IVP: London

Baxter J.W. *Does God Still Guide?* Marshall, Morgan & Scott: London, 1960

Brierley F. *Act on the Facts* MARC: London, 1992

Carlson D. *The Will of the Shepherd* Harvest Ho:Eugene, OR, 1989

Coder S.M. *God's Will for Your Life* Moody Press:Chicago, 1946

Copland G. *God's Will for You* KCP Publications: Fort Worth, 1972

Cunningham L. *Daring to Live on the Edge* YWAM: Seattle, 1992

Dayton E. & Engstrom T. *Strategy for Living* Gospel Light: Glendale, 1976

Devine J. *Find God's Will for You. A Journey with Jonah.* Gospel Light: Glendale, 1977

Dinnen S. *How are You Doing?* STL/WEC : Bromley/Gerrards Cross, 1984

Dobson J. *Life at the Edge (A guide to a meaningful future)* Word: Dallas, 1995

Douglas J.D. *He Loves Me* Here's Life: San Bernardino, 1982

Duncan M. *Move Out!* STL/MARC: Bromley, 1984

Eaton C. & Hurst K. *Vacations With a Purpose* Navpress: Colorado Springs, CO, 1992

Elliott E. *A Slow and Certain Light* Pickering & Inglis: London, 1973

Elliott E. *Discipline, The Glad Surrender* Fleming Revell: Tarrytown, NY, 1982

Ferguson S.B. *Discovering God's Will* Banner of Truth: Edinburgh, 1982

Fitzpatrick G.*How to Recognise God's Voice* Spiritual Growth Books: Fairy Meadow, 1984

Foster R. *Celebration of Discipline* Hodder & Stoughton: London, 1980

Goldsmith E. *Getting There From Here* MARC/STL: London/Bromley, 1986

Goldsmith M.& E. *Finding Your Way* IVP/STL: Leicester/Bromley, 1987

Goldsmith M. *Don't Just Stand There* STL : Bromley, 1976

Griffiths M. *Don't Soft Pedal God's Call* OMF: Singapore, 1970

Griffiths M. *Give Up Your Small Ambitions* IVP: Leicester, 1970

Grubb N.P. *Touching the Invisible* CLC: Ft Washington, 1940

Hansen C. *Knowing God's Will* Group Publications: Loveland CO, 1990

Hay I.M. *Now Why Did I do That?* SIM: Scarborough ON, 1977

Howard J.A. *Knowing God's Will and Doing It* Zondervan: Grand Rapids, 1976

Huggett J. *Listening to God* Hodder & Stoughton: London , 1986

Hughes S. *Understanding Guidance* CWR: Sunbury Mddx, 1990

Jauncey J.H. *Guidance by God* Zondervan: Grand Rapids, 1969

Matzat D. *The Lord Told Me, I Think* Harvest Ho: Eugene OR, 1996

Merton T. *Spiritual Direction & Meditation* Clarke: Wheathampstead, 1975

Meyer F.B. *The Secret of Guidance* Moody Press: Chicago, 1996

Meyers G. *World Christian Starter Kit* WEC/STL: Gerrards Cross/Bromley, 1986

Mumford B. *Take Another Look at Guidance* Logos: Plainfield NJ, 1974

Myers W.& R. *Discovering God's Will* Navpress: Colorado Springs CO, 1980

Ortlund A. *Fix Your Eyes on Jesus* Word: Dallas Milton Keynes, 1991

Packer J.A. *Knowing God* (chapters 9,10,20) Hodder & Stoughton: London, 1973

Poonen J. *Where Do I Go From Here, Lord?* Tyndale Ho: Wheaton, 1971

Sangster W.E. *Does God Guide Us?* Hodder & Stoughton: London, 1934

Simms E. *A Christian's Guide to Discovering God's Will* Hodder & Stoughton: London, 1965

Sproul R.C. *God's Will and the Christian*
   Tyndale Ho: Wheaton, 1984

Swindoll C.R.*Improving Your Serve* (chapter 6)
   Hodder & Stoughton: London, 1981

Taylor R.S. *The Disciplined Life* Beacon Hill:
   Kansas City, 1962

White J.W. *The Race* (chapter 19) IVP: Leicester,
   1984

White P. *Get Moving!* Anzea: Surrey Hills NSW
   1976

Willard D. *In Search of Guidance* Regal Ventura:
   CA, 1984

Weiss C. *The Perfect Will of God* Moody Press:
   Chicago 1950

Training Institutions of WEC International

AUSTRALIA
Worldview Centre for Intercultural Studies
P O Box 21, St. Leonards, Tasmania 7250
Telephone: (0)3 6337 0444; Fax: (0)3 6337 0494
Email: mtctas@vision.net.au

BRAZIL
MTC Latino Americano
CP 289, CEP 39400.970, Montes Claros, Minas
Gerais
Telephone: (0)38 223 3696; Fax: (0)38 223 3742
Email: mtc@amem.org.br

CANADA
Gateway: Training for Cross-Cultural Service
21233 32nd Avenue, Langley, BC V2Z 2E7
Telephone: 604 530 4283; Fax: 604 530 7192
Email: RBryn@compuserve.com

HONG KONG
Missionary Training College of Asia
P O Box 62089, Kwun Tong Post Office, Kowloon
Telephone: 2362 1934; Fax: 2362 1943
Email: asianmtc@asiaonline.net

NETHERLANDS
Cornerstone Centre for Intercultural Studies
Hagelkruisstraat 19, NL-5835 BD Beugen
Telephone: (0)485 36 13 14; Fax: (0)485 36 27 77
Email: 101507.2223@compuserve.com

NEW ZEALAND
Missionary Training College
21 College Drive, RD1, Taupiri 2171
Telephone: (0)7 824 3417
Email: nzmtc@clear.net.nz

WEC International has around 2000 workers drawn from over 50 countries in nearly 70 countries of the world. From its beginnings in the Congo in 1913 it has grown to work in many parts of the world. Evangelical and interdenominational in outlook, WEC's ethos is based on Four Pillars of Faith, Sacrifice, Holiness and Fellowship. WEC's commission is to bring the gospel of our Lord Jesus Christ to the remaining unevangelized peoples of the world with utmost urgency, to demonstrate the compassion of Christ to a needy world, to plant churches and lead them to spiritual maturity, and to inspire, mobilize and train for cross-cultural mission.

To help us achieve that, we have 16 Sending Bases scattered throughout the world which recruit, screen, send and help support workers. We also train missionary workers at six training institutes around the world.

WEC workers are involved in almost every type of direct outreach and support ministry related to the fulfilment of these aims. WEC's ministries range from the International Research Office that produces the prayer handbook *Operation World,* through the planting and establishment of churches, to the enabling of national missionary sending agencies in mature WEC fields.

Our Lifestyle
- We fervently desire to see Christ formed in us so that we live holy lives.
- In dependence on the Holy Spirit we determine to obey our Lord whatever the cost.
- We trust God completely to meet every need and challenge we face in his service.
- We are committed to oneness, fellowship and the care of our whole missionary family.

Our Convictions:
- We are convinced that prayer is a priority.
- We uphold biblical truth and standards.
- We affirm our love for Christ's Church, and endeavour to work in fellowship with local and

national churches, and with other Christian agencies.

- We accept each other irrespective of gender, ethnic background or church affiliation.
- We desire to work in multi-national teams and are committed to effective international co-operation.
- We recognize the importance of research and responding to God's directions for advance.
- We believe in full participation and oneness in decision making.
- We value servant leaders who wait on God for vision and direction.
- We promote local and innovative strategies through decentralized decision making.
- We make no appeals for funds.

If Jesus Christ be God and died for me, no sacrifice can be too great for me to make for Him.   C. T. Studd